THINKING ABOUT PSYCHOLOGY?

Anthony Gale

T·H·I·N·K·I·N·G

ABOUT

PSYCHOLOGY?

Anthony Gale
Professor of Psychology
University of Southampton

BPS BOOKS THE BRITISH PSYCHOLOGICAL SOCIETY

For Liz

BPS Books
The imprint of The British Psychological Society

St Andrews House, 48 Princess Road East
Leicester LE1 7DR UK

First published 1985 by Edward Arnold
(Publishers) Ltd
This edition first published 1990

Typeset by Litho Link Limited, Welshpool, Powys

**Printed and bound in Great Britain by
BPCC Wheatons Ltd**

British Library Cataloguing in Publication Data
Gale, Anthony
Thinking about psychology?
2nd ed.
1. Psychology. Career guides
I. Title II. Gale, Anthony "What is psychology?"
150.20

ISBN 1-85433-031-4

Contents

Psychology's About People

What is psychology? If you have studied psychology at A-Level you will already know the answer to that question, but unlike mathematics, or history or chemistry, psychology is not studied in most schools, and most people have only a vague idea about what psychologists do. Yet for many students psychology seems intriguing and exciting and they want to study psychology when they leave school or sixth form college or take a degree later in life. I wrote this book to help people find out what taking a degree in psychology will be like. It also tells you about careers in the different areas of professional psychology. Most of our knowledge of psychology comes from basic research, and one of my aims is to explain how psychologists study people.

Because the subject is new to you, many of the terms you meet in this first chapter will also be new to you. Don't be put off, because the book has been designed to put over the same message from different angles. By the end of the book you ought to be much wiser about psychology and some of its technical jargon – if not, you have a right to ask for your money back! So please be patient with your author, and don't worry about moving from one chapter to another, because each chapter can be read on its own. You don't need to read the book from cover to cover.

Before we begin, there's a simple mnemonic device (an aid to memory) you can use to help you to remember some key points about psychology. It refers to themes which I return to quite often. Remember the word BASIC. Each letter stands for one of the key areas of psychology: **B**iological foundations, **A**daptation, learning and thinking, **S**ocial psychology, **I**ndividual differences, and applied psychology, or psychology in **C**ontext. If you want to use what psychologists call an external memory aid, you can write the five letters of the word BASIC on each finger of one hand.

BASIC refers to the five ways in which psychologists think about people.

B We are *biological* creatures (we have brains, biochemical and electrical activity in our heads and other parts of our body, and inherit through our genes many of our characteristics).

A From the moment we are born we *adapt* to our environment, and *learn* about the world; we also *think*, reflect on our behaviour, work things out, and solve many everyday and much more difficult problems.

S It doesn't take long for the newborn baby to learn that we live in a *social* world, where other people's reactions to us have a powerful influence on how we feel and how we react. Other people are an important external cause of our own behaviour.

I People *differ* in their reactions and we are not all the same in the ways we feel, act and react. People differ in their personality, their preferences, their talents, their personal beliefs and their social behaviour. Individual differences is a special branch of psychology concerned with how people differ.

C Our understanding of biological factors, of learning, social behaviour, and the ways in which individuals differ can be *applied* in the various *contexts* where human beings work and live. Chapter 4 is devoted to applied psychology.

Psychology and psychiatry. People often ask about the difference between psychology and psychiatry. It isn't possible to give a simple answer, because psychologists and psychiatrists can work closely together. But psychologists and psychiatrists differ in the way they are trained, the ways they tackle problems, the people who are of interest to them, and the ways they find out about people. So, the first difference is that psychiatrists have trained in medicine. Their work is concerned with mental illness and the crises people have when they cannot cope. Trained as doctors, they approach mental illness from a biological point of view, quite often prescribing drugs to reduce patients' symptoms, calming them down before they can help them in other ways. The rationale for this approach is the idea that biochemical changes in the brain may lie behind some mental illness. In contrast, very few psychologists have trained as doctors. Most psychologists are not concerned professionally with mental illness; rather, they want to describe and understand everyday, perfectly normal behaviour. When they do work with psychiatric patients (as *clinical psychologists* do) they are not qualified to prescribe drugs and many of the treatments they use are not based on a biological approach.

Another key difference between psychology and psychiatry is that psychologists are not only keen to study the normal, but think that the abnormal reactions of the mentally ill can only be understood if you first understand *normal* behaviour and normal human development. Finally, psychologists are trained in scientific method and know how to design and conduct experiments and other ways of finding out about people. They use statistical methods to evaluate their research findings. Psychiatrists are very good at listening to what people have to say and this is their most important means of learning about how patients feel. But for psychologists, listening is just one of the ways of studying people.

The scope of psychology

Psychologists are concerned with what makes people tick, *why* they do things and *how* they do things. Anything that people are, or people do, or people think, can be studied by psychologists.

To understand people, psychologists have to know a great deal about quite a diverse range of subject matter.

For the *biological* approach we have to study what goes on under our skin, how the nervous system and other aspects of our *physiology* work. Such research includes anatomy, physiology, and electrical and chemical reactions within the nervous system, from the examination of the action of individual brain cells, to the operation of larger brain structures. Research into the biological bases of our behaviour is conducted both with animals and with human subjects.

The study of *adaptation, learning* and *thinking* extends beyond learning in the classroom to the understanding of the ways in which we handle and remember all sorts of information: how we interpret sensory messages from the outside world to recognize familiar objects, how the child learns to walk, how we learn to use a lathe, or to play ping-pong, how we learn to cope with life's stresses and strains, and how people interact with computers – indeed any context where we acquire new information or new skills or where we develop strategies for dealing with information. Much of what we know about the basic elements of learning is derived from research conducted with animals. Some of the basic principles of adaptation are not unique to the human species.

Much of *social psychology* is based on the study of people in groups and the ways in which people interact and relate to each other, the very social aspects of human experience. This includes studies of interaction between a mother and her child, how people form friendships, decision making in committees, how juries come to a verdict, the behaviour of football crowds, or relations between national and ethnic groupings. The emphasis is on interpersonal behaviour and social influence. Thus psychological research into the family is a branch of social psychology, because the family is a special group, governed by particular rules, relationships and expectations.

Studies of physiology, learning, and social behaviour are carried out in order to describe *general laws* or principles which govern human behaviour and experience. In contrast, the study of *individual differences*, in intelligence, personality, and emotional responses, explains what makes people react in different ways to life events. It helps explain, for example, why some people become mentally ill while others cope with life's problems. Again, if the psychology of learning has general laws about how children learn to read, the psychology of individuals will help us understand why some children learn very quickly and why others experience great difficulty. Intelligence, personality and aptitude tests have been developed by psychologists to assess differences between people. Social psychologists have theories about how groups of people behave and how we are affected by social situations. But they also want to know why some people are gauche when meeting others, or even fearful of social encounters. We differ in our social poise and our ability to form friendships.

Basic knowledge acquired through scientific research into the nervous system, learning and thinking, social behaviour and individual differences, is put to work in real-life situations by *applied psychologists*. One of their goals in their professional life is to enhance the quality of our lives and make us more effective individuals. They apply psychology in a wide variety of contexts.

Wherever there is professional concern with human needs, you are likely to find psychologists at work: in schools, factories, primary medical care, psychiatric hospitals, sheltered workshops, community service, remand centres and prisons. Psychologists tend to want life to be better for us all. They would like to help people overcome their anxieties and disabilities, perform effectively at work, establish satisfying relationships and realize individual talents and potential to the full. That is a very ambitious programme of change, and psychology has not been an established discipline for very long. So enhancement of the human condition is a pretty tall order and we have a long way to go.

However, psychologists already know a great deal about people, and have a good grasp of some of the methods and techniques necessary to study people, groups of people, and their problems. They also realize that people's own behaviour (for example, smoking, drinking, casual sex) can lead to major health problems. There is good evidence that some methods devised by applied psychologists are very effective in helping people and changing their behaviour.

There is a constant interchange between basic research, application, and applied research. Psychologists working in the field apply basic psychological knowledge to help with human problems. They never forget their roots in psychological science. They are aware that the extension of our basic knowledge is essential to understanding people. So applied psychologists keep in touch with developments in other areas of psychology. Also, they are keen to know whether the ways they help people are really effective, and this involves the same painstaking and systematic thinking which psychologists use in basic research. The evaluation of the success of psychological interventions is very complex and a real challenge. Real–life situations involve all sorts of influences on an individual's behaviour, while in the more artificial context of the laboratory it is easier to control how an individual is affected.

The key areas of psychology

Our BASIC mnemonic was used to give you an initial mental peg to hang some key ideas on. Let's be more specific. This is the point where we have to introduce you to some psychological jargon. The following list gives the principal topics studied in first degree courses. The list is expanded in Appendix B. The *only* way you will really get to grips with what all these terms mean is to read more psychology. Appendix A gives suggestions to extend your reading. But there is no alternative to setting out the contents of a first degree, and given that it takes three years to obtain a degree it is hardly surprising if some of the following items seem strange and alien to you. Please skim through the five key areas a couple of times to give yourself an initial flavour. I return to many of these topics in later chapters.

The biological bases of behaviour. Biochemistry and electrophysiology of the central and autonomic nervous systems; the senses; how signals are coded in the brain; physiological bases of 'drives' (hunger, thirst, sex); the emotions (anger, fear, aggression); genetic origins of behaviour; neuropsychology and the effects of damage to the brain; consciousness and sleep; the effects of drugs.

Adaptation, learning and thinking. Classical (Pavlovian) conditioning; instrumental (Skinnerian) learning; short- and long-term memory; complex memory; human learning; language, thinking and problem solving; the role of attention; decision making; artificial intelligence; the measurement of subjective experience.

Social psychology. Mother–child interaction; attraction between people; small groups and leadership; attitudes, values, beliefs and prejudice; conformity and obedience; how others influence our behaviour; peer group influence; intergroup relations; cross-cultural psychology; social behaviour and communication in animals.

Individual differences. The self and self-knowledge; intelligence; personality; aptitudes, interests and special talents; anxiety, response to stress, and coping styles; psychopathology (causes of mental illness); subnormality and handicap; addiction and substance abuse; delinquency; psychometrics and test construction.

Applied psychology. Educational psychology; clinical psychology; occupational and industrial psychology; prison psychology; environmental psychology; psychotherapy; behaviour modification; health psychology; the evaluation of psychological interventions.

Psychologists study people. But what are people?

That sounds a strange question and the answer must surely be obvious, because anyone reading this book is a person and has been surrounded by people ever since birth. You could carry out a simple exercise now, and ask a dozen people to write out the answer. Would they all say the same thing?

The first thing to learn about psychology is that nothing is as simple as it seems. Most of the things psychologists study are *everyday occurrences*, because of course they study what people do, think, and feel.

A common response to psychological research is 'why spend money to find out what everybody knows already?' That is a cross which psychologists have to bear; people studying other subjects, like physics, chemistry, accountancy or archaeology seem to be dealing with very technical subject matter. So you would be rather cautious about telling a chemist that anyone with common sense knows all about chemical reactions. But much of psychology is concerned with everyday experience, about which most people think they are experts. The truth is that many of the things we find out in our research are quite opposite to what 'common sense' tells people, and contradict what '. . . everybody knows already'.

And everyday experience can be taken for granted. For example, most children learn to speak and hold conversations, without any difficulty, by the age of two and a half. So many people take it for granted that such a complex skill happens apparently without much effort. They are only concerned and seek professional advice if a child *fails* to learn to speak. But psychologists do not take such things for granted: they ask how a child manages to master such a difficult task, they analyse language and speech and show just how complex a business speaking is. If we ask how psychologists have studied language and how people learn to speak we can start answering our question: 'what are people?'

Let's study a simple example, of a child learning to make sense with words. It will show how people have to be looked at in several ways at once, following all our five key areas of psychology: physiology, adaptation and learning, social behaviour, individual differences, and applied psychology.

The brain is a good place to start. We know that certain brain areas are intimately related to speech and language, and that even though the child does not speak at birth, parts of the brain are programmed to respond to *speech-related experience*. So, to understand speech we have to understand aspects of brain function. A great deal has been learned about language and the brain from studying language defects in people who have suffered damage to the brain, say, as a result of a bullet wound or a stroke. Damage in different parts of the brain appears to affect different aspects of language and speech.

For example, damage to certain parts of the brain can produce some strange consequences: a person may be able to use a comb and even describe how you comb your hair, but not be able to remember the word 'comb', another patient may recognize bacon from hearing and smelling it as it cooks, but not by seeing it, yet another might be able to write down several coherent sentences, but then not be able to read them back!

But when talking of how children learn to speak what do we mean by saying they respond to 'speech–related experience'? Words, sounds, other people speaking? That is only part of the story, for the interaction between parent and child, even when there is no direct evidence of the presence of speech itself, is part and parcel of language acquisition. Playing, teasing, peekaboo games, rocking and singing are all good fun, but they also set the stage for speech and language later on.

Language is part of our social interaction with others, it depends on the quality of social interaction, and in its turn, it influences relationships between people. In order to speak one has to understand that there is another person to listen to and that they too have things to say. It is in their relationship with their parents that children first learn of their own identity and of the existence of other people. So the social interaction between caretaker (often the mother) and the child is a fundamental part of language acquisition. Psychologists have studied interactions between child and mother and have shown it is a complex process in which each influences the behaviour of the other. Smooth interaction between mother and child involves various components: attending to the other person, taking turns, not rushing, listening, and watching. Such interaction patterns are like a complicated dance for two and, like a dance, it takes time to learn the steps.

The ways parents talk to their children may be influenced by their own level of education, and this in turn may affect the child's mastery of language. This means that the way in which the child learns to talk may be influenced by broader social variables, like the occupational status of the child's parents. A great deal of research and controversy has focused on the relationship between social class and the child's capacity for language.

But language is not just a set of complex sounds or exchanges of sounds between people. Language is used to convey ideas, requests, intentions and feelings. This brings us to the relationship between language and thinking. Let me try to demonstrate how complicated that relationship could be by giving what appears to be a simple example.

A young child says 'I want my ball!' To be able to say that, the child has to be able to recognize balls from other objects like dolls or toy trains, to recognize a particular ball, to have a sense of ownership and to have learned that other people respond to requests (this involves processes of *perception, concept formation* and the development of a *sense of self*).

For the sake of this example we shall focus on the ball. You might wish to claim that the child has an image or picture in his or her head of the ball, and has learned to attach a label ('ball') to it. We could suggest that the brain is like a computer which takes two things from its memory banks, the mind's picture of the ball and its label ('ball'), and outputs them at the right moment. But even a simple round object like a ball proves to be complicated in psychological terms. Compared with a chair, for example, it is simple from a visual point of view, because it stays the same shape from whichever angle you look at it. But it can change colour in different light, and if it is thrown towards you it seems to maintain its actual size, even though the image projected on the back of the eye is smaller when the ball is at a distance. So a ball does change in terms of visual experience. (The fact that a ball looks the same size, even at a distance, is called the phenomenon of visual size constancy.)

But why limit ourselves to vision? We can all recognize the sound of a ball bouncing on concrete or being hit by a bat, we have felt pain if hit by a ball travelling at speed, we know that a rubber ball and a plastic ball feel different both in terms of texture and temperature, and a rubber ball has a distinct smell. The child has to *integrate* and associate *information* from different *senses*.

The child soon learns that balls are used in ballgames; this means running after a ball, judging where to stand to catch a ball (quite a complex problem in ballistics), or kicking a ball in the right direction (the development of *motor skills*).

Balls are personal property, and a visitor to your house may bring you one as a present. You can be playing in the park and discover that large dogs can find balls attractive and run off with them, or puncture them with their teeth. Receiving presents makes you happy (*positive emotion*); losing them can make you angry (*negative emotion*).

There are books with pictures of balls and ballgames, in which special symbols are used to represent balls and other objects in the world. The child will learn to write the word 'ball' and that one may construct many sentences with the word 'ball' in them, like, 'the man kicked the ball', or 'put the ball in the box', or 'all balls are round', or 'this ball is bigger than that one' (the process of *language acquisition*).

If when older the child joins a sports team, balls acquire a new connotation, for ballgames are played by groups of people, and different ball players have different skills and styles of play. Players also react differently to success and failure. Team members and supporters experience a sense of personal commitment to one particular team. In the changing room or on the journey to a match people behave differently from when they are at home. So the child learns about *social behaviour, individual differences in skill and emotional response, social influence* and the *social rules* which apply in different situations.

Are we closer to understanding what people are?

So a simple idea like 'ball' can have complex psychological implications. Somehow we have to integrate information from vision, hearing, touch, taste, smell and pain to make up the concept of 'ball'. Because we have seen different balls (in our own or other people's toybox, or in shops, or on the television, or in different games) we have to be able to distinguish balls of different size, colour, texture and ownership. But information from vision and memory needs to be integrated with other information. For there is also muscular information relating to movements in the vocal tract when saying the word 'ball' or bodily movements associated with ballgames, or hand movements when writing or drawing. We can read, write or say the word as well as kick or throw or catch the object. We can understand the rules which govern where the word 'ball' can and cannot appear in a sentence (e.g. 'the boy was kicked by the ball'). We can understand rules which govern ballgames. We can remember incidents which occurred when playing football, table tennis, or catch; such incidents may be associated with happy or sad memories. They will also be associated with particular people we know and the ways in which they reacted on particular occasions.

Somehow, all this information is capable of being integrated and elaborated in the child's mind, so that the word 'ball' can be used in the right contexts.

This description of the concept of 'ball' and how it develops as the child gains experience is far removed from the notion of a simple image and a simple label. What does it tell us about people? In this description we have talked about physiology (eyes, ears, vocal tract, hand and body movements, parts of the brain), the distinction between self and others, memories for objects and events occurring in different places and at different times, emotions or feelings associated with past memories, knowledge about physical properties of objects and their behaviour in space, the development of our knowledge over time and the elaboration of simple concepts into complex forms, social relationships, and social contexts, rules about language use, rules about ownership and rules about play and games, and the influence of peer groups and special situations.

Psychological method

The example I have given of a child learning to use the word 'ball' is designed to demonstrate two things: that psychological descriptions cover a variety of ways of looking at people, and that psychological descriptions can prove to be more complex than a layperson might imagine, or than 'common-sense' ideas might tell us.

But the example could have been constructed from an armchair, just by thinking about the problem, and not by making any formal observation or carrying out much experimental work.

The words 'systematic' and 'scientific' have been used several times already without explaining what they mean. Psychology is an empirical discipline, which means that psychologists prefer facts to mere opinions, experiments to armchair speculation, precise measurement rather than guesswork, and careful argument rather than mere assertion. In this sense, psychology is like a science and much of our psychological knowledge is based upon facts derived from experiments.

Any claim about how people do things, or why, needs to be backed up from factual information. Facts are obtained as the result of careful observation and measurement. Just like scientists in other sciences, psychologists have developed a large number of special tools for observation and measurement. These tools have been tried and tested in a variety of contexts to make sure that they are reliable and that they measure what they claim to measure. For example, a ruler made of soft elastic would not provide very reliable measurements of length. Similarly, the tools which psychologists use have to be developed with great care to ensure that they are reliable and do the job they are designed for.

Some examples of special psychological tools are: sensitive amplifiers for measuring the electrical activity of the brain, experimental chambers for studying how animals learn, paper and pencil tests for measuring personality and intelligence, questionnaires for measuring social attitudes, event recorders for storing information about mother–child interaction, and a variety of special procedures for measuring the accuracy of vision, hearing and taste. If you study psychology to an advanced level you will find that there are special technical manuals and handbooks describing how such instruments have been developed and the rules which govern how they need to be used to reveal facts in a reliable fashion.

Measurement is one part of the experimental method. If you have followed a course in science in school you will know that an experiment needs to be designed very carefully. The experiment has often been described as 'putting a question to Nature'. The sort of answer you get to a question depends very much on the nature of the question itself. The design of experimental studies is considered in detail in Chapter 3, together with a description of undergraduate research experiments and projects, and the form that an experimental 'write-up' or report can take.

Personal explanations: can people tell us how they think and feel?

There is a very special feature of psychology which makes the problem of measurement different from that in all other sciences. We can *observe* people, and we can take *physiological* measurements from them (for example, recording parachutists' heart rate to see how anxious they are before jumping from a plane). Observation and physiological measurement are not unique to psychology, however. What is unique is our measurement of people's thoughts and feelings, and the explanations people give us of why they do things. No other science is so concerned with *subjective experience* and personal response.

The business of measuring human reports is complex for a variety of reasons. First it assumes that people are good observers of their inner selves, and that in giving a report, they read off information as would an engineer from a dial. The second problem is that we do not accept that people actually have much access to goings-on in their own nervous system. For example, I pointed out earlier that judging where a ball will fall involved complex ballistic calculations. We can use a computer to simulate human estimations of where a ball (thrown at a particular angle and velocity) will fall, and also simulate the movements (and adjustments) people make when running towards a falling ball. A good applied mathematician can then construct equations to fit the simulation.

Now it is probable that within the brain similar calculations are performed all the time and at rapid speed. But the individual is not aware of them – a tennis player simply runs to meet the ball. Thus, we are not fully conscious of many of the processes which regulate our behaviour.

Another difficulty is that people often give *reasons* for doing things which are more to do with how they think they *should* behave, than with what actually happened. It is not fair to say people are not truthful, because the accounts they give of their actions may seem quite genuine to them. But sometimes, other people are better observers of us than we are ourselves. Someone can be blushing yet still insist they are not embarrassed!

The problem of our capacity to introspect, or look inwards, is a longstanding problem in psychology. The measurement of *introspection*, that particularly human ability, raises many problems. Yet it would be a very funny description of people which did not refer to how they describe themselves, their thoughts, feelings and images of actions and events. Unfortunately, the problem of measuring subjective response and the difficulty of interpreting what people say about their inner processes led psychologists to neglect introspection for several years. More recently, new attempts have been made to tackle this difficult part of psychology. For example, we know that mental practice, such as practising your golf swing in your mind's eye, can actually improve your performance. Introspection is so unique to humanity that no study with any other species can help us to understand it.

But we can say that theories of motivation, or what makes people do the things they do, cannot be based just on the reasons people give for their actions. Brought up since childhood to give accounts of our actions, we are used to saying 'I did that because . . . '. But do we really know why? Or have we learned that certain explanations are more acceptable than others? Do we tend to say things that we think others would like to hear or which portray us in a good light? Perhaps we are no better at explaining our own behaviour than we are at explaining other people's? Such issues are considered again in Chapter 5.

2

What is it Like to Study Psychology?

Undergraduate courses

Most universities and a large number of polytechnics and colleges of higher education offer degrees in psychology. Appendix C indicates where psychology can be studied in the United Kingdom and Eire and tells you about the length of the courses and the emphasis of the department (for example experimental, social or applied). The latter can be worked out by looking at lecturers' research interests, the degree course titles, particularly when they refer to special branches of psychology, and the postgraduate courses available. Many other details are also given.

How to choose. If you are filling out an application form you should obtain as much information as possible about individual courses and departments *before* you commit yourself to applying for a place. Your decision needs a lot of thought and preparation. While reference sources in Appendix A and Appendix C are a reasonable guide, the only really up-to-date source must be the department itself. The response you receive to a request for information (i.e. grades required for entry, the selection procedure, the course structure, options available, and a specimen reading list) may offer some indication of the sort of place in which you could be spending three years of your life.

It is important to remember that by joining a department you are entering a sort of educational contract in which you satisfy entry requirements and commit yourself to three years of hard work, while the department should be committed to creating a suitable environment in which to learn and to offering you the best qualification which its resources permit.

Learning and studying on a degree course is very different from learning at school or college. You are expected to do a great deal of work on your own. You have to decide what to study, when to study, and how to study. No one will stand over you. It will be assumed that you are a competent and independent person. Nevertheless, departments do vary in their willingness to assist you in organizing your work, and if you feel you need a lot of pushing you are advised to find out what the department's attitude is in this respect.

Don't always believe what people tell you. Beware of stereotypes about differences between universities and polytechnics, old and new universities, and differences between different institutions. In the final analysis, you yourself will be on the receiving end of what any particular department has to offer; therefore you should equip yourself with any information which is relevant to your response to a particular department.

University or Polytechnic? What do I mean by stereotype? You may have been told that universities are in some sense superior to polytechnics and colleges of higher education as places in which to spend the years of your degree course. My view is that so far as psychology is concerned, other variables are far more important.

For example, all polytechnics have course validation procedures, to make sure courses are up-to-date and well taught. This means that the staff in a polytechnic department of psychology are required to spend time planning their curriculum, justifying their degree scheme, considering options available to students, and evaluating their assessment procedures. Students take a part in this process and, as customers or clients of the department, can express their views both internally and externally.

While some may condemn such procedures as time-wasting bureaucracy, they do at least guarantee that consideration has been paid to the overall structure of the course and the needs of the student.

Universities do engage in consideration of courses, in less formal ways, and most departments will have a *staff–student liaison committee* where students can express their views. But unfortunately, there are some university departments where there has been little change in courses over the years.

In order to qualify eventually as a Chartered Psychologist and to gain entry to the postgraduate courses described in Chapter 4, the undergraduate course you follow must confer eligibility for membership of The British Psychological Society and give the Graduate Basis for Registration as a Chartered Psychologist. It is essential that you confirm that the course you propose to follow is adequate for this purpose and has been approved by the Society. People may tell you a course is innovative and exciting or that it offers a high degree of choice, but it will be of little value to you if it contains a poor sample of psychology courses. So if you want to become a psychologist, make sure you ask the department concerned about the status of their degrees *before* you commit yourself.

Campus or City? Another stereotype of relevance to any degree course is that of the 'campus', or 'red brick', or 'grey brick' institution. You may entertain all sorts of ideas of what it is like to work and live in one, and may think that campus life in a provincial university somehow captures the delights of the older universities. Roughly speaking there are major institutions set in the middle of large cities, and campuses set out of town, either with residential accommodation on site or some miles away. You may be someone who is happy living in a cloistered community with all your needs (shopping, banks, laundry, entertainments) catered for within a square mile, or you may be happier walking to your lectures through bustling city streets. It is essential to talk to people who are already students at the institution so that you can discover if it meets with your own particular needs. A campus can be as lonely as a big city for some people.

What type of degree? The majority of psychology degrees are of three years' duration. In Scotland, most degrees involve four years' study, with a progressive development of specialization. Three-year degrees and Scottish degrees start with basic course material covering the areas specified in Chapter 1 and Appendix B, with more specialization and choice of optional courses in the final year. Optional courses vary from department to department.

The sandwich degree. There are four-year degrees in psychology which allow for a sandwich year (a year of practical experience), made up of two placements each of a term's duration, or a single full-year placement. There are variants for sandwich provision, but sandwich placements are most likely to occur in your third year, once you have acquired sufficient knowledge of psychology and psychological method to enable you both to appreciate the work being done in the placement and to contribute to it. Departments attempt to place their students in a practical context (research unit, hospital, factory, educational unit, clinical unit, special residential home, administrative unit) where professional psychologists are employed. The local person acts as a day-to-day supervisor, and a teacher from the parent department will pay regular visits to consult with the student and the supervisor.

Local education authorities will usually allow a year's grant for this purpose, but some placement supervisors are able to offer employment at a modest salary.

Such sandwich arrangements are attractive for several reasons: you experience the practice of psychology in a real-world context, you have experience of full-time work, the temporary placement could possibly turn into a full-time post after graduation if the local supervisor is impressed with your skills, and you are of course, more mature and older at the time when you take your final examination. You may also have real experience of conducting experiments or acquiring expertise in special psychological techniques, which will stand you in good stead for your own final-year project work. Some four year degrees, with special sandwich placements, confer accelerated eligibility for some forms of professional practice.

At times of full employment, a sandwich year could be seen to offer disadvantages, since it could mean the loss of one year's salary, or a later start on your career path. It is impossible to give general advice on this issue, and some sandwich placements prove to be more beneficial than others, but they do enable you to have references from someone who has seen your performance and competence in a working situation. If you fancy a sandwich year, try to find out what special arrangements the department has to prepare you for the placement and to supervise you at the time.

Which faculty? Generally speaking, it makes little difference whether you obtain a science, social sciences or arts degree. The first determinant of which course you follow could well be the types of subject you have studied at A- or AS-Level. The core subjects of most degree courses are pretty much the same.

The differences lie either in ancillary subjects taken or in the subject chosen for a combined honours degree, if such an option is preferred. One can study psychology with a wide variety of combined honours subjects (for example, sociology, philosophy, physiology, statistics, business studies, biology), the choices available being dependent upon the options offered within the university or polytechnic.

There are two cautions that must be attended to. A general guideline is that the psychology components must be at least 50 per cent of the degree course content and that the degree must give the Graduate Basis for Registration for you to be able to continue with a career in psychology after graduation.

A second caution is that combined honours degrees are notorious for the hard work they entail, for they often seem to contain most of the core of two separate degree courses. The ideal combined honours degree is one where the teachers in the two departments concerned offer joint courses, to assist you in bringing the two disciplines together. Such an approach ensures that you can exploit the two disciplines to the full and make them enrich each other. But there is a danger that a combined honours degree student feels a second-class citizen, or displaced person, without a home in either department.

In most institutions, it is possible to change your mind and switch between courses during the first year of the course, so that a decision to follow a single honours or combined honours course need not be irrevocable, so long as the alternative to your initial choice actually exists. For example, a student could register initially for a combined honours degree in psychology and sociology, and then switch later to a single honours degree in either subject, so long as there are places available and the tutor thinks the reasons for changing course are sound. Alternatively, the institution *may* offer other combined honours courses, say in psychology and philosophy, or psychology and statistics.

Choice of ancillary subjects. There are two points of view about ancillary subjects. The first is that you should seek to study a subject which has a bearing upon psychological theory or research, or the application of psychology. Typical examples of such courses might be physiology, animal behaviour (taught by a biologist), biochemistry, philosophy, computing, business studies, or sociology.

Such subjects, because of a potential overlap with psychology are said to be 'cognate' But it is a matter of good fortune whether you are able to link the two disciplines in a coherent fashion. After all, a student studying psychology only as an ancillary subject is unlikely to plumb the depths of the discipline.

The other approach is to make a very conscious selection of a subject which is interesting in its own right and has no apparent relevance to your psychology course, say archaeology, or the history of art, or a language, or music. You will have noticed that the distinction I have drawn between 'cognate' and 'not relevant' is a hollow one: for music, art and language are things people do and psychology is about what people do. Sure enough, there is psychological theory and research about music and aesthetics, for example.

The truth is that the links between your ancillary and main subjects are for you to develop. If you are a passionate musician, and have the opportunity to follow a course in music as an ancillary subject, you may well decide to carry out a research project on the psychology of music. Or, you may decide that your music and your psychology can be kept apart.

What makes for a good department? If you are keen to follow a career in psychology after completion of your degree, then a very important consideration is whether the staff in the department concerned are themselves respected members of the profession. Clues to their standing are the number of research grants and contracts they have been awarded by the research councils, government departments and industrial companies; the number of full-time postgraduate researchers; books published and papers published in learned periodicals; and whether the department has special units for applied psychology or postgraduate courses leading to further qualifications. Such information can be directly obtained from the department concerned.

While many of these activities seem to be outside the concern of the undergraduate, they actually impinge on teaching and career prospects in a major way. For example, while most courses have similar material during the first two years (this is discussed in detail below) the final year tends to be one in which you can follow advanced options. Teachers who themselves are actively engaged in research and are pushing forward the frontiers of knowledge, are likely to offer very authentic and up-to-date teaching at this stage; people who get their hands dirty in the hard graft of research have a much fuller understanding of the problems involved than someone dealing with the material at second hand.

Such considerations also apply to your final-year project, which can be enhanced by association with an active research group or an applied psychology group. The project is a major element in your learning and your final degree assessment, and it is of benefit to be supervised by someone who is in touch with the subject matter in a direct way.

Again, tutors responsible for postgraduate courses (if they exist in the department) can offer good advice on how to prepare for a career in, say, educational, clinical or occupational psychology. You will need informed advice on how to make an application for entry to such a course when you graduate (see Chapter 4).

Finally, it is worth enquiring whether the department has regular visits and lectures by academics and practitioners from the outside, and whether there is a student psychology society which has a full programme of visiting speakers. All these factors are good indicators of the environment offered by a department.

What qualifications do you need? The grades required for entry at A- and AS-Level could be more a reflection of university or faculty policy, or the competition for places, rather than a direct indication of the quality of the individual department. If psychologists are keen on A-Level grades, then they are either ill-informed or misguided, because they are very poor predictors of subsequent performance, even in degree subjects which are similar to those studied at A-Level. Nevertheless, there is some evidence that a good grade in GCSE maths and a pass in a science A-Level can help you to get a better psychology degree.

There is typically no special requirement as to the subjects to be taken at A-Level, although the subjects taken must be acceptable by the institution's general regulations for entry. This lack of insistence upon special subjects reflects the fact that psychology may be studied within science, arts or social science faculties, and may be combined with a variety of other subjects (which may themselves have requirements – see Appendix C).

But because of the importance of statistics in all psychology courses, a pass at GCSE mathematics is usually mandatory.

The selection process. Very few psychology departments engage in lengthy selection procedures. Some departments do have specially devised procedures including mental tests, personality tests and interviews.

The most likely outcome of an application, if you are a school or college leaver, is that you will be offered a place subject to obtaining certain grades at A- and AS-Level, that is, if your school record indicates that such success is likely. A visit is frequently then offered to enable you to make your choice.

A good quality visit will enable you to see the campus as a whole, visit residential accommodation, provide a guided tour to the department, provide information about course structure, and offer question-and-answer sessions with both staff and students. It will also take place during the term rather than during vacation, so that you can sample the place as it will be during your own time as a student.

If you are a mature student there is a chance that you can be offered a place without special additional qualifications, following an interview designed largely to determine your grasp of what a psychology degree entails and your motivation to undertake the course. But courses accepting mature students typically require some evidence of recent successful study.

What can you expect to see on a visit? I am now going to take you on a brief tour of an imaginary, but not atypical, psychology department. This will serve two purposes: it will help you to have an idea of what to expect, and it will help me to tell you more about psychology as a discipline.

I am prejudiced enough to believe that psychology departments have one thing in common: they are generally friendly places, the staff are typically approachable and not unduly pompous. It is very difficult to teach people in practical classes, seminar groups and tutorials without getting to know them pretty well. A friendly and helpful environment offers a good context for undergraduate study, because the going can often get tough and it is reassuring to know that sympathetic people are at hand.

The laboratories. The physical fabric of psychology departments is likely to have a number of common features. Most have a large special-purpose laboratory area. You will not see benches with bunsen burners or sinks; rather, the general teaching laboratory area is likely to have loose chairs and tables and cupboards for storing equipment. Banks of microcomputers are commonplace. Practical work early on in the course tends to be carried out in large groups.

As you acquire more expertise, experiments may be carried out in small individual cubicles large enough for two or three people and an item of apparatus. Quite often, students carrying out project work may have one of these cubicles allocated to them and if possible, you should approach them and create the opportunity to ask them about their research.

Look for notice boards around the building and in the laboratory classroom and read the notices; these will give you a flavour of how the department is organized. Some notice boards are chaotic, others organized and friendly, while some are replete with instructions, exhortations, and stern warnings!

Two other essential areas in a department are the workshops, where technical staff prepare equipment for teaching and research and develop computer programs, and the departmental office. You should find that technical and clerical staff take a pride in the efficient running of the department and are happy to give advice and assistance.

Animal laboratories. Some departments have specialized animal laboratories. It is unlikely that you will be able to visit these except in very special circumstances, as very strict regulations govern the running of animal laboratories. The most popular laboratory animals are pigeons and rats, and there are one or two departments with primate sections.

The social psychology or observation laboratory. Another common feature in most departments is a laboratory with three areas: an observation room large enough for groups to sit in, with a one-way screen to an experimental room (again of reasonable size) together with a control room for video monitoring. Advanced suites will have remote-controlled cameras and a variety of mixing procedures, for example, the capacity to show the faces of two people talking to each other (split screen).

But, unlike normal television studios, a psychology suite will also have special timing devices to impose a clock on the videofilm and computer-based systems for recording what happens on the film. These observation rooms can be used for a variety of purposes: watching children at play or solving problems; studying people's behaviour in small groups; administration of individual intelligence tests (where the presence of observers in the room might distract the person taking the test); role play (for example, a surgery consultation between doctor and patient); or an interview with a disturbed person, who would be distressed by the presence of anyone but the clinical psychologist interviewer.

Some departments have such observation facilities attached to a creche or nursery school, where for both teaching and research purposes children may be observed engaging in spontaneous play, or carrying out special experimental tasks, without the distraction of an outsider.

Computers. Most departments have a range of computing facilities. Psychology has made a great deal of use of the minicomputer and more recently there have been major investments in microcomputers, often in network arrangements.

Computers are used in four ways. Some departments do include a compulsory course in basic computing for all students. This is particularly helpful if you have no prior acquaintance with computing, or have anxieties about computing.

But computers, particularly in networks, are more frequently used for teaching statistics; they enable students to work either during class hours or in their own time.

The most likely use of computers is for presenting experimental material; for example in memory experiments, material to be learned can be presented in a very flexible fashion by using a computer display, and computer displays can offer good control over material in the field of perception. For example, in face recognition experiments, a picture of a famous person can be altered in a variety of ways to see which cues to recognition (such as hair, eyes, mouth) are the most important.

Again, networks may be used for classwork, or individuals may work at particular experiments, either as a subject or as an experimenter, in separate cubicles. The computer will not only present information to the subject, but store a record of responses and accumulate the data for subsequent analysis. For example, the subject, in a reaction time study, may have to press certain keys (say in response to one of five light stimuli). The computer will record speed of reactions, and plot the distribution of responses for each subject. It can then be programmed to accumulate the information gained from a number of subjects and combine it with a view to statistical analysis (for example, are people quicker in responding to one light out of three rather than one from five, or do people instructed to be accurate rather than fast make fewer errors?).

A final use of computers is for complex data analysis, for example, the analysis of complex physiological signals, like electrical signals from the brain. This particular use, for analysis of analog signals, is more likely to be found in association with research or advanced undergraduate work.

In some departments computer displays may be used as an interactive notice board for giving you general information, for example about where lectures are to be held, availability of reading material, old examination papers and so on. Computers can also be used to present complex material on visual display units or via video systems, as an aid to lectures and demonstrations. And some psychologist love producing aesthetically exciting 'live' or dynamic displays for teaching purposes. A lot of material in psychology lends itself to visual effects.

The introduction of computers has made a major impact on psychology departments, which have been quick to exploit their potential. Indeed a great deal of valuable psychological research has been carried out on problems of interaction between people and computers, the 'friendliness' of computer dialogues, and the ease with which programs may be followed by users. A major research area is in artificial intelligence, where computer programs are used to simulate several psychological processes, and problem solving and thinking in particular.

Is there somewhere to talk? A final feature common to many departments is a room called the 'seminar room', or perhaps 'special teaching laboratory' which often proves in fact to be a student common room or a place where staff and students can drink coffee and talk to each other in an informal or relaxed atmosphere. The informal encounters and discussions in an educational establishment are probably as important or even more important than the more formal timetabled period of instruction.

Specialized facilities. We have probably reached the point where generalizations about the physical fabric of psychology departments break down. Staff usually have their own offices where you will meet for consultations about your work or for small group teaching. They are also likely to have their own research laboratory, which will be equipped for their own research work.

For example, my own research is in human physiological psychology or psychophysiology, and my laboratory has a polygraph or multi-channel recording system which enables me to record electrical activity of the brain (from the surface of the skull), heart rate, skin conductance, muscular responses, respiration and blood pressure. I have a special-purpose computer for analysing these biological signals and a multi-channel tape recorder for making a permanent electrical record. My experimental subjects sit in a separate sound-deadened room and many of my experiments involve them working on information-processing tasks, my aim being to observe bodily changes during learning. Some psychophysiologists have devices which enable them to monitor bodily activity while people walk about doing their normal daily tasks. Such systems are particularly useful in monitoring people in factories, or athletes during sports performance.

My laboratory reflects my own research interests. Here is a sample of other special-purpose laboratories which my colleagues have developed, to give you an indication of the range of activities undertaken: a 'wired-up' crib to study activity and sleep-wake cycles in newborns, a grand piano linked to a computer so that complex keyboard skills and the way the brain programmes serial motor movements can be studied, a computer interface for monkeys to enable them to press keys to indicate items of food they want, a whole-body vibrator to study the response of passengers to vehicle vibration, a rotating chair to study motion sickness, a simulated motor car driver's cabin with computer projected windscreen and normal motor controls, a special laboratory to study the effects of lighting levels and types of fluorescent lamp on interpersonal behaviour, a simulated office with computerized documents and personal information on clients, a large maze for studying spatial orientation in monkeys, a mobile laboratory which can be taken to schools or factories or used for filming pedestrian behaviour at road crossings.

Staff working on special projects of their own are often keen to involve students with their work, and want to talk about their own research as often as possible.

Who are the staff? The people who teach you are very likely to have worked in an academic environment for most of their working lives. Having obtained a good degree in psychology, they will have devoted a further three years or so to research and the preparation of a doctoral thesis and the award of a PhD or D.Phil. There is a further discussion of what a doctoral dissertation entails in Chapter 4.

They may then have entered teaching immediately or have spent time working as a post-doctoral fellow attached to a particular research project or research unit. When appointed to their teaching post, they probably had the expectation that they would be able to call upon their authoritative knowledge in their chosen area of research for at least part of their teaching duties.

There are of course many deviations from this model. Some staff will not have a doctoral qualification, some may have trained as professional psychologists, taking a master's degree course in clinical, child, educational or occupational psychology; this is particularly likely in a department which has a strong emphasis in the direction of applied psychology. It is also very likely that you will have the opportunity to be taught by psychologists whose main employment is outside the institution. In some places it is possible for your project work to be supervised by a clinical or educational psychologist. Some people teaching in psychology have other qualifications, say in engineering, or philosophy, or some branch of medicine. Such colleagues add a very special flavour to a department, because they are members of it yet see psychology from another point of view. The courses they offer, if they draw upon expertise acquired in another discipline, can be quite unique and refreshingly different in style and viewpoint from other courses on offer.

Students do sometimes become confused about what particular

academic titles mean. In the UK the term 'professor' usually applies to the most senior members in a department, while in North America this is a general term applied to teachers in higher education. Some professors in the UK are appointed as administrative heads of departments, or to an established Chair, while others are elected to personal professorships because of the excellence of their research.

Finally, it should be said that many staff have not been able to move to new posts in other institutions; whatever people might wish to do, there is little incentive for such a move. Unlike many other professions, there are few opportunities in academic life to improve your working conditions and salary by a job change. Combined with the absence of new teaching posts, this has had the effect of increasing the average age of your teachers, and the unfortunate effect of reducing opportunities for the appointment of female staff. You will find that while some 70 per cent or more of psychology students are female, many departments have very few female staff. If such matters are of importance to you then you should find out what the position is before making your final choice of department.

I have devoted a good deal of space to describing the context in which you study for a degree in psychology because context is often of considerable importance, particularly if you are going to develop a sense of commitment to your chosen subject. I am also aware that many potential students have a rather woolly idea of what the study of psychology involves and what the habitat or natural ecology of the modern–day psychologist looks like.

We now look at the content of courses in more detail.

What are the course components? Most courses are very similar in content during the first two years. There are essential parts of psychology which all students must become acquainted with. Courses may vary in terms of the time allocated between psychology and other disciplines, particularly in the first year. By the end of the second year you are likely to have studied a good proportion of the following subjects or course units: the biological bases of behaviour, learning, memory, child development, sensation and perception, social psychology, comparative psychology, psycholinguistics, cognitive psychology, consciousness and attention, personality and intelligence, psychometrics, motivation and emotion, and psycho-pathology or abnormal psychology. These are seen as the main substantive areas within the discipline and you will discover what each topic covers by reading Appendix B and examining one of the introductory textbooks suggested in Appendix A.

Departments vary in the degree to which they phase these subjects and the amount of time they allocate to each. This can depend on the particular interests and training of the staff within the department. Such emphases can give a department a characteristic flavour, for example, make a department more 'biological' or 'social' than others, and you would be wise to ensure that your own particular interests have an opportunity to flourish.

The majority of the subject matter in psychology is based upon empirical research; this means that it is really impossible to have a deep understanding of any area of psychology without a grasp of the principles of experimental design and at least some elementary statistics.

In addition, therefore, to the above list of subject areas, most courses will offer lectures and problem classes in statistics throughout the first two years. There will also be a weekly practical class in which you yourself will conduct empirical work. A good proportion of this work will be based on experimentation, but it will also include other psychological research techniques, such as observational studies, interviews, administration of psychological tests, role play and simulation. The next chapter gives more detail about these activities.

At this point it must be emphasized that in my own experience, the majority of students who drop out from psychology courses do so because of a misconception about the nature of the subject and in particular, a failure to recognize the importance of the psychological method and the need to become competent in experimental design and statistics.

As psychology is taught more and more in schools, such misconceptions are likely to diminish, but they can lead to considerable distress for a student who fails to realize that they are likely to have not only to conduct empirical work but to hand in detailed practical reports on a regular basis.

The main differences in course content between psychology degrees lie within the final year. Some courses are lecture based, others are centred upon seminar groups and optional courses, where much of the effort in preparing for teaching sessions must be expended by the student. But the main source of difference is likely to be either the overall emphasis of the department, or the research interests of staff.

In the former category, there are degrees whose title includes a particular reference to applied or occupational psychology; here the final-year emphasis will be upon the application of psychology. The majority of courses, however, include some options in applied topics, but treat applied psychology more as a postgraduate study than as an undergraduate study. For example, an undergraduate course in abnormal psychology will be more concerned with the causes of mental illness and the disturbances it may create in our behaviour (for example, language disorder or disruption of social relationships in schizophrenia) than with diagnosis, treatment, or the practicalities of rehabilitation.

Because courses on offer for the final year tend to reflect the research interests of staff, no department can guarantee in advance that particular courses will be available to you in your final year, as it cannot be predicted which staff will be available. However, you are likely to be offered some choice, and the work you will then do could very well be at the frontier of knowledge in that particular field. Thus a psychology degree is attractive in taking students without prescribed qualifications and bringing them up to a high level of competence within three years.

Some regard the final-year project as the highlight of the psychology degree. This is an opportunity for you to work on a topic which you have selected, in considerable depth. Sometimes, a student can make a personal contribution to the development of the discipline as a result of the findings of their project. A full description of the experience of doing a project is given in Chapter 3.

What if I have a handicap? There is nothing about a psychology degree which would exclude students with sensory handicaps or handicaps which necessitate use of a wheelchair. So long as you have the required entry qualifications, departments will be happy to enrol you and to make any necessary arrangements to ensure that you enjoy your degree course to the full. Institutions vary in the facilities made available, but they are typically conscious of the fact that people with a handicap have not received provision in the past. Some buildings can prove impenetrable to a wheelchair and some library shelves are not always easy to reach. Most institutions will ask you to see their medical practitioner or their special adviser on disability, to ensure that all difficulties can be anticipated. In any case, it is essential that you make an extended visit to the institutions of your choice, to ensure that all will be well for you. It is very important that there are practising psychologists with handicaps, because they can help to change public stereotypes about disability.

Psychology as an ancillary subject

You may be a student who has registered for a degree in a completely unrelated subject and have discovered that you are required to follow an ancillary subject for two years. What can psychology offer you? If you have read much of this book so far, you should have a reasonable grasp of the nature of psychology.

Many universities and polytechnics offer psychology as a first-year option, and it has proved to be particularly popular in Scottish universities. Ancillary courses are likely to be of an introductory nature, covering the full range of psychological study, but of necessity in a relatively superficial fashion. Since psychology is about human behaviour, and most of us are interested in people, you should find such a course stimulating and challenging.

If you are uncertain, in spite of what you have read so far, you could spend some time usefully examining one of the introductory texts mentioned in Appendix A.

Some of these introductory courses include a practical class component; this tends to give you a better feel of psychology, since practical experience takes you beyond the scope of material read secondhand in a textbook. However, one year of study is unlikely to offer more than a brief sample, and you will need to follow up particular topics, either as options in later years, or in private study, if you wish to have a good grasp of the area, or indeed, wish to discover its relevance to your own main subject of study. Psychology has recruited a number of excellent students who began initially as students in other disciplines.

If you have taken a course in psychology at A-Level you are likely to find an introductory course to be lacking in challenge.

Psychology as part of professional training

Psychology is about people. It is not surprising therefore, that psychology should play a part in the training curricula of professionals who have a major concern with the health and welfare of people.

Psychology is an essential component of a variety of courses in professional training, including medicine, nursing, health visiting, speech therapy, occupational therapy, physiotherapy, psychiatry, social work, teaching, management and police work.

Psychology is applicable to these professions in three ways. First there is psychological theory and research in relation to the populations with whom the professional works and with the contexts in which they work. Thus nurses would need to know about the psychology of pain, childhood, the aged, the mentally ill, handicap, the effects of bereavement on patients and their families, and institutional life. This would include special study for example, of memory deficits in the elderly, or individual differences in the experience of pain.

Secondly, there is a body of psychological knowledge about professional practice which is relevant to the development of personal skills. The nurse needs to know about principles of learning and teaching, about communication with patients, and about studies of the effects of psychological preparation of patients for operative procedures. Such knowledge should have a direct effect upon the practice of nursing and patient care.

Finally, there is psychological knowledge concerning the development of self-understanding, and appreciating one's own motives, one's prejudices and preconceptions, all of which might influence relationships with other professionals and with patients or clients.

We can summarize these three ways in which psychology is relevant as: basic knowledge, knowledge about skills, and knowledge of self. The particular emphasis which the tutor will place on these components may be affected by the official syllabus, local requirements, and the previous experience of the tutor. Probably the best tutor for such courses is someone who has direct experience of the profession in question. For example, a number of nurses and teachers have taken degrees in psychology at some time in their career. The combination of psychological knowledge and specialist professional knowledge can be particularly powerful.

Those of you who are proposing to take an undergraduate course in psychology and who are reading this section should note that application of psychology in relation to the practice of other professions is increasing all the time. Indeed, within the medical and paramedical professions there are psychologists practising behavioural medicine and the sub-specialty of health psychology. (The broader term, behavioural medicine, can include disciplines other than psychology such as medical sociology, epidemiology and community medicine.)

The health psychologist need not necessarily be a clinical psychologist, trained to work with psychiatric patients. For example, a social psychologist might be involved in changing young people's attitudes to sexual behaviour in the context of HIV infection. An occupational psychologist might conduct research in a general hospital to examine the effects of shift work on nurses' health and efficiency. The demonstrable value of psychology in helping other professionals get to grips with psychological problems in their field of practice, and the capacity of psychologists to suggest new ways of doing things, has created many new opportunities for psychology itself. Further reference to this development is made in Chapter 4.

Studying psychology at school

Psychology may now be studied at A-Level, and some examination boards offer psychology at GCSE and AS-Level. It is of historical interest that early attempts to introduce psychology in schools were blocked because it was feared that it was somehow 'unhealthy' for people to study psychological processes in themselves or others. Such misconceptions die hard. Even relatively recently, I have seen very derogatory comments on students' applications to my university, made by their headteacher along these lines: 'This is a very bright student who has the strange ambition to study psychology' . . . or . . . 'A difficult and argumentative student, clearly suited to psychology'!
. . . 'A difficult and argumentative student, clearly suited to psychology'!

Psychology has in fact proved to be a very popular subject in schools, both for science and non-science students.

In the UK, the Association for the Teaching of Psychology is a very active and effective organization with a membership predominantly of Advanced-Level teachers. The examining boards have had to make a difficult choice as to what to include and what to exclude from A-Level, AS-Level and GCSE syllabuses. Some syllabuses are extensive in scope and cover the full range of psychological knowledge; in this respect they are not dissimilar in content from first-year introductory courses at universities or polytechnics for people taking psychology as an ancillary subject.

Some syllabuses allow some specialization in the second year, following a general introductory first year. One course focuses on child or developmental psychology, but uses theories and experiments in that area of psychology to illustrate general features of the discipline. It is possible to focus on child development and sample most of the psychological methods (including experiment, observation, interviewing, psychological testing, and physiological monitoring).

All courses demand familiarity with the experimental method and some elementary statistics.

The International Baccalaureate examination has three syllabuses in psychology. The Subsidiary syllabus focuses on the work of a set of famous psychologists, and teachers can choose from a list of possibles, so long as the work of the psychologists they have chosen covers a variety of approaches (biological, behavioural and humanistic psychology). The Higher Level syllabus includes in addition a choice of options for study in depth and requires students to conduct three individual research projects, using different psychological methods. There is also a Higher Level syllabus in experimental psychology, which includes options for study in depth, a laboratory course, and individual project work.

This variety of available syllabuses and a number of syllabuses under development, reveals that psychology is still a growth subject. Contrary to the views of earlier critics, the complexities of human behaviour and experience can be studied in a meaningful way by students who are still in school.

The British Psychological Society awards an annual prize to the candidate with the best A-Level performance for those examining boards which offer psychology.

As psychology is taught and examined at school level, more people will learn what psychology is about and what professional psychologists do. One problem for me, as author of this book, is that knowledge about psychology will soon be so commonplace that the book will become redundant!

3

The Discipline of Psychology

Every discipline can claim that it teaches the student two things: a body of systematic knowledge, unique to that discipline, and a set of specialist skills. In the last chapter I explained what a psychology department is like as a place to work in, and sketched briefly some of the key features of undergraduate courses.

I am now going to make a very strong claim for psychology and say that it is in a very special and advantageous position in relation to other disciplines. Because psychology spans science, social science, and arts approaches, it samples a wide variety of intellectual and practical skills.

Thus psychology shares a number of skills in common with other disciplines, but it has the advantage of *combining* them in a way which is unique. Psychology combines literacy, numeracy, ways of thinking, and practical skills which no other discipline brings together under one umbrella. This has two consequences.

Firstly, like graduates from other disciplines, psychology graduates are rather special people; they have learned to think and do things in special ways. Just as a chemistry graduate or a graduate in languages has special skills and knowledge which no one else has, so the psychologist is rather special.

But unlike graduates from many other disciplines, the potential for *applying* the skills they have acquired, across a broader range of intellectual, working and personal contexts, is considerably greater. That is to say, a psychology graduate is a very employable person because he or she is so well equipped across the board.

A good way to describe a psychology graduate is as a good problem solver. When one considers that psychology courses do not typically demand specialist requirements for entry (other than a pass in GCSE mathematics) then the capacity to produce a well–rounded individual with broadly applicable competence is a considerable achievement. Whatever the disciplinary background of students when they enter psychology, they finish their degree course with first-rate marketable skills.

A first degree in psychology does not qualify the graduate for employment as a professional psychologist. The various paths to professional qualification are considered in the next chapter. At present only a small proportion of graduates (something in the region of 10 per cent) is able to enter postgraduate training courses; successful candidates are likely to achieve a high degree class (at least a Class IIi) and to be able to demonstrate practical experience of relevance to clinical, educational or occupational psychology. Thus there will be a large number of psychology graduates who cannot entertain hopes of entering the profession. Therefore, at a time when employment prospects are not generally buoyant, the marketability of the knowledge and skills acquired during a psychology degree course must feature in any decision about whether to study psychology or some other subject.

I have spent most of my working life in psychology, and therefore have a strong sense of commitment and enthusiasm for my discipline. I think it has its own *intrinsic value* and is worth studying for its own sake. Like other psychologists I have a sort of obsession about learning about people.

But nowadays there is a definite bonus in a discipline which not only offers a good education, but an additional benefit for potential employment prospects. While I love psychology for its intrinsic merits and believe in the pursuit of knowledge for its own sake, I do not feel ashamed to say that psychology is *useful* and *applicable* and that psychology graduates are potential applied scientists and excellent employees. Don't forget that most problems in life and most working situations contain a major human element. Skills in understanding people, observing people and working with people must surely make us more effective. What are the skills which a degree in psychology will teach you?

Literacy

From the very first week of an undergraduate course you will be invited to read original articles in learned journals, or to tackle books which extend beyond the scope of general introductory texts. Indeed many psychologists in the UK have a distaste for general introductory texts because they see their necessarily superficial approach as selling psychology short. A department might recommend that you purchase an introductory text *before* joining the course, to ensure that you obtain a good overall view of the nature of the subject.

But you will find that unlike many other subjects, you are encouraged very quickly to use the library in an active way and to purchase specialized texts. Good students build up their own private library very rapidly. This must mean that to make the best of what you read, you must develop a facility in reading quite complex material and in obtaining information from it. It is also likely that you will be asked to write essays or to prepare written material for tutorial or seminar presentation. Again, you may well be criticized for basing your written work on elementary texts or for plagiarism. So the demands for competence in literacy skills are imposed very early in the degree course and persist throughout the course. Indeed, since most courses place a progressively greater responsibility on students to work on their own, an ability to read, to understand, to make sensible notes and to organize one's developing fund of knowledge, is quite essential. Reading and understanding are *active* processes. You are unlikely to remember the contents of a book merely by skimming through it. Students develop different strategies for extracting information and imposing their own organization on it. To read well, you have to ask yourself questions and check that you have understood the author's arguments.

Not only is it necessary to write essays but there are additional specialized demands in relation to report writing (see page 45). So, by the end of your degree, you should be capable of reading and understanding a wide variety of material, of putting other people's ideas into your own words, and of writing lucid and coherent prose. Such skills do not come easily to most of us, but a great deal of practice, with the benefit of feedback from your tutors, will help to overcome a variety of writing handicaps.

I can also promise that the business of reading and writing gets easier with practice, for a variety of reasons. At first a book is like a rich jungle to you and the list of contents seems a poor map to help you hack your way through. But soon you begin to build up 'cognitive maps' of psychological knowledge, internalized represent-ations of what you are learning. These structure the material and help you identify and make sense of things seen in the jungle, and you begin to recognize the flora and fauna. By the end of your final year in psychology you should be able to pick up most books, have a rapid sense of the subject matter they cover, and be able to pick out and select aspects relevant to your current learning and writing tasks. Mastery allows selectivity and discrimination. And because you have begun to focus on aspects of psychology which suit your interests, and lay aside (if not fully discard) topics which do not excite you, the task of reading and selecting is one of pleasure and fun.

Some courses allow you to prepare a dissertation on a topic of your choice. This can prove to be a great voyage of discovery and some students can produce dissertations which are true works of scholarship; they capture a problem in psychology and illuminate it, reveal a thorough grasp of the appropriate literature, and perhaps synthesize material in such an original manner that they help to reorganize part of our psychological knowledge. This can be the very height of your reading and writing experience in psychology and gives you a sense of personal ownership and participation.

Of course, other disciplines offer such intellectual and personal rewards, but psychology has yet more to offer.

Playing with ideas and theories

There are theories in every branch of psychology, and most empirical studies are designed to test a very specific hypothesis which is derived from a theory, or which sets up the predictions of one theory against the predictions of another theory. In every lecture you hear and in every book you read, you will have to think very hard.

Theories are not just loose bundles of ideas but have a number of formal properties. The first property of theories is that they specify a part of psychological knowledge which they seek to explain, for example, 'the development of language in young children', or 'the behaviour of people in groups', or 'how we see colour', or 'the causes of satisfaction and dissatisfaction at work'.

Theories then focus on a set of explanatory concepts, which are related to each other in a formalized fashion. In Sigmund Freud's famous theory of the structure of the mind, there are key concepts such as id, ego and superego, and these structures are related in certain ways and in accordance with rules or principles which the theory specifies; for example, the ego is seen as an executive arm of the id and has to employ a variety of techniques (including mechanisms of defence) to maintain stability of the individual. (A worked example of the operation of defence mechanisms is offered in Chapter 5, where I consider possible causes of idleness in relation to individual study!)

So one of the first problems which can arise with theories is whether they actually do manage to explain the phenomena they seek to explain and whether the key concepts in the theory do hang together and relate to each other according to the rules which the theorist sets down. Looking at the formal structure of a theory to see if it hangs together in a way which is coherent and free of contradictions can be hard intellectual graft.

But psychology goes beyond theory to observations and measurement; the theory has to be tested in the real world. A good theory therefore tells you what steps you have to take to test the truth of the theory and see whether it fits the facts. Much of psychological knowledge is therefore based on experiments which have been set up to test particular theories and your lectures are likely to focus on the ways in which a particular theory has been tested and whether the results of experiments are compatible with the claims which the theory makes. This imposes quite a demand on the student, because you have to ask yourself a great many questions about everything you read. For example:

▶ What exactly is this theory about?
▶ Do I understand the key concepts and what the author means by them?
▶ Do I understand the rules which govern the relationships between concepts?
▶ How does this particular hypothesis, which is being tested, arise from the theory?
▶ What method is this experimenter using to test the theory and why?
▶ Does the design of the experiment really test the theory in the best possible way?
▶ Do I understand the results of this experiment?
▶ What bearing do the results have on the original theory?
▶ Could there be alternative explanations?
▶ Is there another theory which can explain these results any better?
▶ Will the theory have to be adjusted or even discarded as a result of this experiment?
▶ Are there other experiments whose results are compatible with the theory, or contradict it?
▶ Can I devise a better experiment to test the theory?

These are just some of the questions you will have to ask every day, and as you read psychology and listen to lectures. By now you should have captured what I mean by saying that you will have to learn to 'play with ideas'. The sort of procedures and processes which I have mentioned are part and parcel of what we call the *discipline* of psychology. By the end of your course you should be able to recognize a good theory and know what makes a bad theory inadequate, to examine evidence in favour of a theory, to think of new ways of testing a theory. Indeed, the project which you are likely to carry out as part of your final year work will enable you to play an active role in the testing of a theory which interests you. Once you have experienced playing with ideas and theories you will become a sceptic. You won't accept what you read in newspapers or hear on radio or television. You will learn to ask the right questions, and know what sort of evidence could be necessary to offer an appropriate answer.

This is a sensible point to issue a warning. Psychology is an empirical discipline, and theories are tested by formal observation and experiment. If you feel uncomfortable with the ways in which experimental scientists think and work, then you may well find the typical undergraduate course in psychology unsuited to your particular style. Such warnings have to be given because a major reason for the small number of dropouts from psychology courses seems to be that students experience a shock when they discover how much practical and experimental work is involved.

If your studies in school or college have included experimental work, then you will know what to expect. But those with an arts or social science background are strongly advised to cross-examine themselves on this issue and read some experimental psychology before making a formal application to study a psychology course. I am not saying that only people with a science background do well in psychology. That is simply not the case. But to do science you have to appreciate what it involves. Most introductory texts will give you a clear idea of what practical research involves.

Listening

It may seem strange to suggest that you have to learn to listen. Because of the nature of psychology and the ways in which it is taught, systematic listening skills, are essential. Unlike many science and mathematical subjects, a lecture in psychology is not simply a means of conveying complex information from one head to another.

In some subjects, a good series of lectures serves as a reasonable substitute for a good and authoritative textbook. Students may find that they are writing down a great deal and that they need to study their notes that evening in order to ensure full comprehension. It is a rare psychology lecture which involves continuous writing down of material presented on a display (chalkboard or overhead projector) or of the precise words uttered by the lecturer. An ability to write shorthand, or to transcribe verbatim what has been said, is unlikely to be helpful.

Listening in a psychology lecture is likely to be an active rather than a passive process; much of the material can be understood without great difficulty, but it is essential both to concentrate on the material and to restructure it for your own purposes. The aim is both to understand the material and to record the important or salient features.

Many of the questions which are listed above in relation to getting to grips with theory and experiments need to be constantly on your lips. So your lecture notes should contain additional material, over and above what the lecturer says, recording doubts, worries and questions about some of the things the lecturer says or omits to say. Statistics lectures in psychology have a special additional requirement. Because statistics is logical and sequential in structure, each step needs to be understood before the next step is tackled. This means that to get the best from your lectures in psychological statistics, you must not only concentrate during lectures, but ensure you have thoroughly understood the work before you attend the next lecture. This may include working through recommended examples; quite often with statistical problems you need to work the example before the principle clicks home.

Similar methods of listening apply to tutorial and seminar sessions, when the speaker is likely to be a fellow student. There you will need to listen so that you yourself can make a relevant and meaningful contribution to the development of the material under discussion. Your lecture notes, or notes taken at a seminar meeting, are never likely to be sufficient for your thorough knowledge and understanding of the topic under discussion; you will need to carry out a great deal of further reading and exploration of the literature.

If you are the sort of person who likes a relatively passive approach to learning, you may find that psychology does not have sufficient structure for you. Good psychology students learn to structure the material themselves. Most reading in psychology is like a continuous question–and–answer session, the reader needing both to challenge the material which is presented and to test their own understanding. Strangely enough, this involves listening to yourself! A good way of testing your own understanding is to hear yourself give a mini-lecture on a topic; is your version comprehensible, and does it make sense? And as your knowledge develops, you will also need to *relate* what is being read to what you have already learned.

Such skills are of course required in many disciplines and are not unique to psychology, but the interaction between learner and information in psychology is, in my view, more similar to social science thinking than to traditional science thinking. The material tends to be much more complex much quicker; that is to say, early on in the learning process the going can get tough. For in every field of psychology there are few *facts* which are not subject to challenge.

Numeracy

I have mentioned statistics several times, without trying to explain what the term means. You can think of the numeracy that a psychology student acquires by calling it 'playing around with numbers' just as earlier, we talked of playing around with ideas. Psychology is a quantitative discipline, that is to say, it emphasizes measurement and the mathematical modelling of events.

'Events' mean a range of psychological data. These may include measurement derived from a variety of instruments, including human judgements. Here is some work for you to do. As you read the next paragraph have a piece of paper handy. Note down each example I give, and then decide whether you think the *measurement* involved in the example is likely to be *hard* or *easy* . Then say why.

Here are some examples: heart-rate responses during proof reading (measured by a polygraph), reaction times in a complex choice situation (measured with a millisecond clock or timer), teachers' rankings of children's social behaviour (based on teacher judgements of children in their class), frequency of mutual smiling between mother and infant during breastfeeding (based on event recorder analysis of a videofilm), aesthetic judgements of abstract paintings (derived from presenting pairs of paintings to subjects and asking them to choose their favourite), verbal descriptions made by airline pilots of what they do when taking off or landing (taken from tape recordings during flight), self-deprecatory statements made by depressed patients at early or late stages in treatment (taken from clinical tape recordings), diaries of a participant observer describing life with a streetgang (written by the observer after the events occurred), or an account of a fire given by five different people (interviewed in hospital shortly after the fire).

You can see by looking through the list that some of these data look more dependable or robust than other data sets.

Time estimates (reaction time) or physical measurements (heart rate), seem different from records of mutual smiling (mother and infant) or judgements of social behaviour (teacher ratings). And how do you analyse the content of a diary (gang observation) or the pilot's commentary (real-time recording); how do you assess a 'self-deprecatory comment' (patient's talk in therapy): are some worse than others, and how do you count them? These different types of measure fall into three different types of scale: *interval, ordinal* and *nominal*. The type of measurement derived affects what you can do with the numbers. Part of the fun in psychology is to devise ingenious ways of measuring human experience and judgements.

But measurement is a servant of theory. In the examples given, we may have made certain predictions from theory. For example, that heart rate is faster when reading more complex typographical proofs (the reverse is actually the case!), that speed of reaction is a function of the number of possible alternatives (the greater the number of possible lights, the slower the response to an individual light), that teachers tend to make more favourable judgements of children who are obedient and conformist, that mother and infant smile more at each other towards the end of a feeding session, that extraverted subjects prefer brighter, less complex and more colourful abstract paintings, that landing a plane is much more difficult and creates more anxiety than taking off, that a skilful therapist (as measured by factors such as empathy and warmth) changes the way a depressed male client talks about himself, that streetgangs have power structures and elaborate rules governing their behaviour, or that people in different parts of a building vary systematically in their report of a fire. Such predictions were made on the basis of particular hypotheses derived from special theories.

Experimental design is about designing your investigation in order to put your question to Nature in a precise and unambiguous fashion. This ensures that the data which emerge are directly relevant to the hypothesis in question and have a clear and direct bearing on the theory under test.

Say there is a controversy about the best way to teach a foreign language. We can set up a study to compare two methods for learning French: the *oral* method (where the emphasis is on speaking the language and on class discussion using the names of familiar objects) and the *formal* method (where written work, basic grammar and reading come first, before practice at speaking). The oral theorist claims that early real-life practice at speaking makes for greater fluency and gives the student more confidence. The theory under test suggests that conditions which are like the ways in which French children learn to speak French are appropriate for English children learning to speak French, i.e. by the oral method. Would it be enough to ask Teacher A to teach Form I by the oral method, Teacher B to teach Form II by the formal method, and then compare the results?

Would this simple experimental design give a clear and unambiguous answer? I shall list some of the problems in the form of a series of questions: are Teachers A and B of similar experience and competence in teaching French? Do Teacher A and Teacher B have a similar and unbiased view of how best to teach French? What was the level of competence in French in Form I and Form II before the experiment began, was it equivalent? Are there differences between Forms I and II which may be relevant, for example, if Form I has a higher proportion of girls, and girls are more successful than boys in language learning, might that not bias the results in favour of Form I? What is the attitude of other teachers in the school towards different methods of language learning? Can we be absolutely sure that Teacher A and Teacher B have used methods different only in relation to the oral/ formal distinction? If we do obtain a strong effect after, say one month, might it be due to novelty, and will it persist for a longer duration? Two things are apparent here. The first is that we might be confounding a test of a language teaching method with differences between teachers or differences between forms. The second is that if we want to design a good experiment then we have to control for any variable which might be a major source of influence on our results.

For example, we might wish to allocate teachers of equivalent experience at random to different teaching methods, or test classes first, and then match classes for linguistic ability before the experiment begins. We might wish to repeat the design across several schools, just in case, for example, some schools are particularly keen on new methods, or particularly resistant to change.

You can consider other ways in which we might improve this design. What you will discover is that your mind is working logically testing out questions like: 'What would happen if we did . . .?' or, 'Might the effect of teachers be different in schools where there is an active involvement of parents . . .?', and so on.

Some designs may seem logical but not particularly relevant. That is where we move from the notion of formal design, to *elegant* design and the *art* of scientific research. Elegant designs test the questions you wish to ask in a subtle yet economic fashion. Some scientists seem particularly good at asking questions in the right way.

The example of language learning was chosen because having to learn a language is something which most readers of this book will have experienced. You may now wish to look at some of the studies you made notes about (see page 40) to see what might be a good design and what factors might be confounded by an inept scientist.

For example, if we take our fire in the building study ask yourself if in certain buildings there may be a difference between staff located near or far from the entrance, a difference which itself might be a source of differences in capacity to give a detailed or adequate description.

Before we leave the language learning example, you might have noted that the theory on which the study was based could have defects in it. Children who learn French in France are much younger in age than those who learn French in the UK and have no language experience or competence when they start. They also learn language in the context of home and in the familiar domestic surroundings which they share with their caretaker. As we saw in Chapter 1, learning your natural language is not as straightforward as it seems. Devising new methods to teach languages is also a difficult business.

I have talked about the most elementary type of research design, and you will not be surprised to learn that, as with other topics I have discussed, there are many textbooks considering a broad range of experimental and research designs in psychology. If you like the feel of numbers, and enjoy thinking in a logical, tight and systematic fashion, you will find such characteristics enhanced by a psychology degree course.

Experimental design is very complex in research with human beings because we are complex and the variables which influence our behaviour are not only difficult to identify, but can interact with each other in unpredictable ways. Psychologists, like other scientists, are very concerned with the notion of experimental and measurement error, the possibility that aspects of the experimental procedure themselves provide unreliable data. For example, several psychologists have questioned the validity of the psychological experiment itself, and the special environments psychologists have devised to conduct their research. Is a pigeon in an experimental box like a pigeon in the wild, is a human subject in a small soundproof cubicle the same as a subject sitting in their drawing room at home? Such issues prove to be part of the fun of designing experiments, interpreting results, and challenging other people's research!

When we get the data from our research study, we need to subject it to formal test, to see if the results are reliable, or could have occurred by chance. A good scientist has a clear idea of what form the data will take before the experiment begins, because design and statistical test work hand in hand. Different statistics are appropriate to different designs.

An important notion is that certain statistical tests make assumptions about how the world works in terms of the patterning of potential results. The test asks whether the particular results obtained could be there by chance or whether there is only a weak probability that such results could have occurred. Statisticians have selected an arbitrary probability level as a minimum condition for wishing to accept a result as better than chance. There is controversy over this as with other aspects of statistics, but one probability commonly accepted in psychology is that the result could only have occurred on less than one in 20 occasions.

But it would be misleading to characterize all psychological statistics in this fashion, since there are many views as to the best statistical model to use for psychological data, whether to have assumptions, and what these might be.

It must also be said that a high proportion of experiments do not always go as anticipated; scientists will have a good idea what their data might look like, but they never blind themselves to looking really hard at the data after the experiment is over. New and unexpected results can lead to new interpretations of theory and new experiments. Some very interesting psychological facts have been discovered by sensitive researchers, quite without prior intention. I almost said 'accidentally', but that cannot be wholly true, for a scientist's training and feel for data enable recognition and appreciation of a new and interesting finding.

If you are frightened of numbers, you need not be. For statistical tests ask logical questions in a formalized way; if you understand the logic, your understanding of a statistical procedure will not be far behind. The results of any experiment you carry out will lend themselves to very straightforward verbal descriptions; the statistical tests tell you which of such descriptions you can assert with confidence. Teachers of statistics tend to be people who have a natural feel for mathematics; they sometimes find it hard to understand how the student cannot follow detailed proofs. Psychology teachers of statistics merely require you to have a pass in GCSE mathematics. They would certainly prefer it if you could follow proofs and the full reasoning behind individual tests, and they certainly will want you to cast all timidity behind you and work hard to grasp your statistics.

But they are psychologists and are professional teachers and so they feel they should be able to get well motivated and bright students to an acceptable level of competence, whatever their prior mathematical or statistical background.

Experimental design and statistics are essential to all branches of psychology, pure and applied, and the formal logic of statistical inference applies in all empirical domains. There are no simple short-cuts to knowledge and merely asserting what you believe with gusto and confidence will not convince a psychologist. Psychologists are such competent people in the health services and in education because they are unusual in having been trained to think about numbers logically and systematically, both in relation to their own work and that of colleagues in other professions. For our example in language teaching we could have substituted a comparison between different types of therapy for depression, or between training programmes in computer use in a factory, or different techniques for teaching handicapped children to dress themselves. Many people have a fair idea of what applied psychologists do, but they fail to realize how much continuity there is between their basic research and knowledge about human behaviour and their practice as agents of change.

Report writing

You should already have an inkling of what a report of an experimental or other psychological investigation is likely to look like. There will be a theory to be tested, a hypothesis or prediction derived from the theory, an appropriate experimental design, a report of results, the application of statistical tests, and a set of conclusions including an appraisal of the theory in the light of the results, and an appraisal of the experiment in terms of its outcome and possible ways of improving it. All these features arise from the proper practice of the psychological method, considered in this chapter and elsewhere in the book. While different departments and different staff members will vary in their requirements, most practical reports will have sections entitled:

Title
Summary
Introduction
Method (including design, subjects, apparatus, procedure, instructions to subjects)

Results (including graphs, tables, rationale for statistical tests, verbal summary of findings)
Discussion
Conclusions
Bibliography

Most degree courses include practical and laboratory work in the first two years at least. You will be required to produce reports on a number of experiments or practical exercises. In some departments these then become part of your formal assessment. But assessment aside, it should now be clear why such reports are part of psychological education, and why, as an education, they offer such a special discipline, combining both the arts and skills of literacy and numeracy.

For example, it may seem strange to you that in the list of items above I mention 'Title'. Constructing a title is actually quite hard since psychologists like titles which are brief, pithy and informative. Again, a summary looks an innocent enough requirement, but actually it is quite a skill to explain in, say, 100 words, what was done, how it was done, why it was done like that, what happened, why it happened, whether it met expectations, what possible measurement error was present, and what (if you are not exhausted) it would be sensible to do next. Indeed each part of a good report makes different demands on the writer and that is why report writing is such a good discipline.

There are many occasions in working life where one has to summarize the state of things in clear language (i.e. give an account of how things are), state what the problems are, suggest possible causes of how they came about, identify objectives and solutions, consider alternative courses of action, compare them systematically, and come to conclusions and recommendations. The psychology graduate, if well trained, should have no difficulty in combining the demands of verbal fluency with those of clear thinking.

The project

Your project is a very special report, because it is your own, it arises from your own interests, it is your responsibility, and you live with it and worry about it for most of your final year. Typically, the project represents a significant proportion of your degree assessment and can be influential in the final degree class you are awarded and the staff's assessment of your future potential after your degree course is over.

The importance of the project can make it overwhelming at first for the student, and one of the most frequent problems is to help students cut down their ambitions to a workable size. In laboratory classes, many of the studies you conduct are designed for you or based on group discussion; this ensures their practicality. Projects can run out of hand and your supervisor (who will usually be an expert in that field of study or in related fields) will guide you without putting ideas in your head. Projects are often typed and bound and look very smart (so long as students proof-read the typing properly!) and students become very proud of their work. But more important, some projects are not only an excellent exercise in learning but can contribute to scientific knowledge, and lead to yet further research.

In line with my claim that psychology combines a wide range of skills, I believe the project to be one of the finest features of a degree course, particularly when the students (now in their final year) are able to draw upon all the knowledge and skills they have acquired so far in the course. When writing references for students, to future employers, I make great play on their project work, for it is an example of sustained effort, on a piece of work they themselves have chosen to do. It is therefore a potentially good assessment of what they might be capable of, if given a free hand and personal responsibility, in the outside world.

Projects are so much fun that they tend to vary considerably, reflecting the skills and interests of students. There are few generalizations that can be made with confidence. However, it is worth pointing out that the organizational aspects and time management can be greater than imagined at the outset. For example, gaining access to a school to study a group of children in an experimental task can take time, and involves special permission and a good relationship with the teachers concerned. Similarly, special equipment for a laboratory-based study can take time to develop. Therefore, planning, anticipation, and a good level of resistance to frustrating circumstances, are always worthwhile attributes.

Matching your science to your own interests

We have seen that project work can arise from your own particular interests in psychology. But we have also mentioned the availability of options, the chance to choose among alternative courses, particularly in your final year. Your tutor will help you decide on the best set of subjects to follow. Psychology, because it is interested in most things people do, also has things to interest most people. For example, if you are a computer buff, you are very likely to be able to work with computers, say in the field of artificial intelligence; if a musician or an artist, it is possible to study salient psychological topics, like keyboard skills, aesthetic judgements, perfect pitch, creativity, or performance anxiety; if you are keen on working with children, people in groups, people with handicaps, then it should be possible to express this interest in your psychological study; if you intend to become a teacher, there is a large range of topics of extreme psychological relevance, for example, cognitive psychologists have developed fascinating models of how we learn to read and write (there are now even theories about spelling!). The truth is that the psychological world is your oyster and that a degree in psychology enables you to extend yourself in a manner which can be personally satisfying.

Working with others

Many of the skills we have talked about so far involve the development of personal competence. In some cases (listening, for example) other people are involved. Most forms of employment do involve collaboration and co-operation with others. Appropriate experience is provided by a psychology degree course in a variety of ways. In practical classes you are very likely to have to work on practical exercises with others, each taking responsibility for different aspects of the task; for example, acting as a subject, controlling the apparatus, and scoring responses.

In some departments it is possible to carry out group projects, where again each individual will have to accept responsibility for particular facets of the work, and the whole group will need to learn to tolerate individual differences in attitude, style of work, and competence.

In final-year work, particularly when it is based on seminars and seminar preparation, every student becomes both dependent on others and depended on by others. Staff members expect students to prepare coherent and well-organized presentations for the group, and are unlikely to step in and rescue someone who, without warning, has simply failed to carry out their undertakings to fellow students and prepare adequately for the meeting. These aspects of sharing, discharging one's role, learning to carry out expected functions, and a sense of tolerance for others, are of course familiar features of working life.

Sensitivity to the influence of values

The psychology student soon learns that the notion of the scientist uncovering essential truths is not a wholly accurate description of the scientific process. Each scientist lives in a period of time when certain ways of thinking are dominant, and where the sorts of question which thinkers put to Nature tend to reflect a dominant view of the world.

Thus the scientist is influenced by the value systems of the prevailing culture and the models of the person which are popular at the time (this is sometimes called the *zeitgeist,* or 'spirit of the times'). In psychology, the consequences can be profound. For psychologists study people, and the contemporary *zeitgeist* will influence the ways in which the psychologist studies people; indeed, psychologists might influence the *zeitgeist* itself by the way they choose to study people.

For example, if the psychologist studies learning in rats, or problem solving in computers, then other people might come to think that people are *like* rats, or *like* computers. Such a way of thinking could lead to the dehumanization of the way in which we all think about other human beings. Thus science is uncovering truths, yet at the same time selective in which truths to uncover, and introducing a source of bias (or measurement error) in the way truth is uncovered. For example, in this book I have tried to avoid using the personal pronoun 'he'. If I had used 'he' it could have created an impression in your mind that all psychology students and all psychologists are male. That is far from the truth of course, but the example shows how even our use of language can influence our world view. Many psychologists claim that too much psychology has been male-orientated in the past; for example, psychoanalysis is seen by some members of the women's liberation movement to have portrayed women as weak, dominated by sexual fantasy, and lacking in moral strength. Psychoanalysis was a predominant and influential model of what people are for more than 50 years.

This is not an easy point to put over. Perhaps one final example will suffice. In a major controversy in the first quarter of the century, British and American psychologists argued over the concept of intelligence, whether it was innate, general, and an all-round ability (the British view), or whether there was a cluster of differing abilities (the American view). Some critics suggested that the British view reflected the British class system and the notion that people were born to their station in life ('the rich man in his castle, the poor man at his gate. God made them high and lowly and gave them their estate'). In contrast, the American view was said to reflect the Protestant Ethic, the notion that in a free society, hard work and endeavour could lead any individual to the highest reaches of society. Thus, it was claimed, the protagonists in this dispute were more affected by the cultures they lived in than they realized.

The problem of values intrudes in all aspects of our lives, and in particular in the field of social services and professional work which involves working for the benefit of other people. The sensitivity of the influence of cultural and other value systems, which psychology students acquire, will stand them in good stead in working life. It will also provide a strong dose of scepticism when politicians or others make statements about what people are or how people should behave; the psychologist appreciates that values change with time.

Conclusion

The thrust of Chapter 3 has been to show how much you can get out of psychology in terms of intellectual, practical and scholarly skills. My argument has been that while individual elements in psychology courses (literacy, listening, playing with ideas, playing with numbers, report writing, project work, expanding upon your own interests within the discipline, working with others, and appreciating the influence of values on our thinking) do have their equivalents in other disciplines, no other discipline has the advantage of combining all these features in one course, and thus educating and training the individual in such a satisfactory and satisfying range of knowledge and skill.

There is an additional feature of psychological research and practice which is essential to any psychological training. Because psychologists work with people they have special ethical responsibilities; these are discussed in the following chapter, for convenience, and not because ethical issues apply more to the application of psychology than to original research.

Finally, I was tempted to suggest that a psychology degree has a further advantage, that of helping you to understand yourself more. I am in the embarrassing position of feeling this is true, but I am not able to offer scientific evidence for my belief! It would require a very special research study, and also a very difficult debate about what it means to 'understand oneself'. In view of my continual emphasis upon rigorous research and satisfactory and robust evidence, I must be cautious. Let me allow myself the indulgence of saying this, that understanding others (having a variety of psychological accounts of how and why other people do things) probably reflects on our sense of what *we* are and how *we ourselves* view the world. If part of a psychology degree is to describe and understand human behaviour, then it seems likely that our own behaviour might be a proper subject for reflection and study.

The emphasis in this chapter has been upon psychology when taught as a degree course. Hopefully, many of the elements I have described will shine through when psychology is taught in other contexts, in both school and in higher education.

4

Psychology Applied

This chapter is about applied psychology and the opportunities which psychology offers for a career as a practising psychologist. Appendix A gives the titles of a number of excellent books published by The British Psychological Society, which describe the different key applied specialties (clinical, educational, occupational, and criminological and legal psychology) in very much more detail than space allows us here. I will describe how one becomes trained in these branches of applied psychology, what sort of work one is likely to do, and specialties which are evolving (community psychology, behavioural medicine and counselling). There are opportunities also for applying and developing what one has learned at undergraduate level within the context of a career in research or teaching. Finally, attention is given to ethical issues which can arise both in psychological research and in the practice of applied psychology.

A model of applied psychology

The scientific approach of psychology, and the testing of theories and hypotheses by experimental means were described in earlier sections. The applied psychologist, even while practising in the field, and under the daily pressure of the demands of work, still remains a scientist. Applied psychology is systematic, makes observations, analyses problems, tests possible solutions and having implemented a plan of action, then seeks to evaluate whether an intervention has been successful or not. These characteristics are common to all branches of applied psychology, and the psychologist is first and foremost a *psychologist* wherever he or she is at work, be it in a hospital, a school or a prison. Thus the names 'clinical', 'educational' and so on, owe more to the context in which the psychologist works, rather than to psychology itself.

In different countries the brief which a psychologist has to satisfy will vary, as a result of public attitudes and historical trends. For example, in some European countries, all schools, whatever age group they cater for, have psychologists as permanent members of the staff (this probably reflects a long tradition of interest in children and in their education and welfare); in the UK the psychologist visits the school when the headteacher makes a special request, usually in relation to difficulties which an individual child is having with learning, behaviour or emotional problems. Some schoolteachers never meet a psychologist. A clinical psychologist is unlikely to visit a school nor, indeed, is a prison psychologist, although some school problems, for example, relating to aggression and violence, look very much like the sort of problem they would be competent to deal with. The fixed pattern of work which a clinical psychologist may satisfy now is likely to alter very rapidly, as the general public appreciates the range across which applied psychological expertise can be appropriate, and practice can vary considerably in different parts of the UK.

Some academic psychologists and some applied psychologists have begun to question whether specialization is very sensible, particularly if it serves to separate the different practitioners, in spite of the fact that they have many skills in common. After all, psychology is about people, and people are still people whether they are children, elderly persons, workers, patients or prisoners. It is worth noting this important point because if you are reading this book with a view to becoming a psychologist in say seven years' time, the picture in the UK may look very different. In my optimistic and more adventurous daydreams, I conjure up an image of a new sort of psychologist. For example, I believe every secondary school has enough work for six psychologists on its permanent staff. Their brief would go well beyond the present focus on the individual child. Among the problems they would be equipped to tackle I include: teacher stress and job satisfaction; management and decision making; organizational change; staff development; the design of classrooms and workshops; changing attitudes about smoking, sex, drugs and diet; vocational guidance; establishing varieties of assessment; sports psychology and training. My dreams may have become a reality by the time you graduate.

It is possible to construct a general job description for applied psychologists as follows, drawing upon undergraduate education, professional training, and professional practice:

The nature of applied psychology

- Psychologists bring about *change* either in individuals or in groups of people.
- Such changes are typically designed to improve *the quality of people's lives*.
- Through their training, psychologists engage in systematic *observation, measurement and report*.
- They are presented with *problems to solve*; these are often multiply–determined and not easy to understand without extensive investigation.
- Society's view of *what people are, their rights and responsibilities* tend to vary over time and the psychologist has to be sensitive to the implications this has.
- Psychologists work in *organizations* usually run by other people and subject to organizational rules and practices.
- Psychologists, by virtue of their training, cannot know how people *should* behave; quite often the psychologist has to find out *what the person wants themself*.
- The clients whom the psychologist meets belong to a number of social groups which are important to them and which influence the ways they behave and think (*their family, workplace, religion, political affiliation*).
- Helping people can be stressful; psychologists have to devise *coping methods* both for themselves and their clients.
- Many psychological interventions involve *training and education*, teaching clients to take *personal responsibility for their own lives*.
- Psychologists have to *evaluate* whether their interventions actually work.
- Psychologists work with *other professional groups* (nurses, doctors, social workers, administrators, managers, prison governors). For their work to be effective, they have to appreciate how colleagues see their own profession.
- Psychologists, as practitioners, are subject to *legal constraints* and new forms of *legislation* might affect the nature of the services they have to deliver to clients.
- Psychologists have to be good, as public servants, in *allocating limited resources* in an effective way.
- Psychologists work with people; this has special *moral and ethical* consequences.

The work of any applied psychologist, whatever the nature of their employment, can be described along these lines. The above list includes reference to: beliefs and ideals, processes, methods, skills, context, responsibilities and attitudes.

Clinical psychology

Following a first degree it is necessary to take postgraduate professional training. The most common form is to prepare for a Diploma or Master's qualification in clinical psychology, over a period of two or three years. Such courses combine theoretical and practical components. For example, trainee clinical psychologists typically spend five or six months working in each of five or six areas of specialty; adult psychiatry, mental handicap, child psychiatry, plus selections from neuropsychology, the elderly, primary medical care, forensic psychology, and other options, depending on local circumstances. During the practice period the trainee is supervised by an experienced psychologist; academic work goes on in parallel.

Examinations include written assessments, case reports, and a dissertation based on an empirical project. Once qualified, clinical psychologists can spend their time dealing with individual patients, in organizations like special homes or accommodation or, as they become more senior, at a planning or policy level within the health services. The range of work undertaken defies a uniform description; it can include individual therapy for depression and anxiety, addictive behaviour and other personal problems, group therapy, assessment of the mentally handicapped, psychological testing of people with brain damage, rehabilitation programmes for long-term patients, assessing whether elderly patients can cope in the home, teaching other professions about psychology (nurses, psychiatrists, social workers), helping voluntary groups in the community, giving advice to the families of patients, and conducting research into the causes of psychological disorders and the effectiveness of treatments.

More and more, psychologists are working within the community; some 30 years ago they were likely to spend most of their time within psychiatric hospitals carrying out routine assessments using mental tests.

Clinical psychology and opportunities for employment are buoyant. However, training places on postgraduate courses are highly over-subscribed. Many courses prefer to ensure that you know exactly what the course entails and what it is like to work as a clinical psychologist.

They will therefore look more favourably at students who have chosen appropriate courses at undergraduate level, have worked in appropriate contexts (for example as a psychiatric nursing auxiliary during the vacation), or have done an undergraduate project, or even postgraduate research, which shows both high motivation and relevant experience.

Many graduates now take up jobs as psychology technicians, working with clinical psychologists on special projects for a year or so. A job like this gives you the opportunity to meet patients and observe psychologists and other health professionals in their natural habitat. Strictly speaking, however, psychology technician posts are non-graduate support posts and the salary is therefore very low.

Educational psychology

The training period is the longest in this case, and is likely to become longer as the amount of knowledge in the field is expanding rapidly. After graduation you must take a Postgraduate Certificate in Education (which lasts one year) and work as a teacher for two years. It is then necessary to persuade your employer (the local education authority) to second you to a university- or polytechnic-based Master's course in educational psychology. (In Scotland, however, it is not necessary to train or work as a teacher before training as an educational psychologist.)

There is one course, in my own department, which is integrated over the four years of training, and which therefore not only finds the person a teaching post following completion of initial teacher training, but keeps in contact with students throughout the four years.

Master's courses are likely to be extended to two years' duration, so if you have taken a four-year degree, it could be nine years in all before you are fully qualified (although you do earn a salary as a teacher and during secondment).

As with clinical psychology, the range of activities undertaken by educational psychologists is expanding. The work includes: assessing individual children and recommending a programme of treatment and education, planning special school curricula, advising parents and teachers on children with handicap or with behaviour problems, advising on learning problems, counselling adolescents with personal problems, giving advice on aspects of school organization including residential schools, devising assessment procedures for use by teachers, helping to train teachers, helping voluntary groups (for example, with the organization of creche and nursery arrangements), and conducting research in all these aspects.

In our general 'model' it was mentioned that applied psychologists have to work with colleagues in other professions; in the case of educational psychology, the general view has been that one cannot understand the life of a teacher or what it means to work in a school, without having gone through those experiences oneself. There is controversy over this issue and at least one official government report suggested that teaching experience was not essential; however, the situation is unlikely to change in the near future.

Occupational (sometimes called industrial) psychology

Here psychologists are concerned with people at work. It is possible to be employed as a psychologist in personnel work, in industry or commerce or even in the government service, without having a further qualification in occupational psychology, particularly if the first degree was applied or occupational in nature and included appropriate sandwich experience.

However there are Master's courses available in either occupational psychology or in human factors or ergonomics, with considerable overlap in content, although the former has emphasis on selection, vocational guidance, the development of assessment and training methods, unemployment counselling, retirement counselling, welfare, staff development and organizational change, while the latter is concerned much more with the interface between people and machines, either at work (computers, production lines, air traffic control, military operations) or in other contexts (building design, vehicle design, special devices for the handicapped).

It is possible to take a Master's course in human factors or ergonomics without a psychology degree (for example, with a degree in computing, or architecture, or engineering). This means that the psychology graduate can experience interaction with intelligent and competent people from other disciplines, exchanging expertise and experience. (Possession of such a Master's qualification in the absence of a first degree in psychology will not confer chartered status – see page 15 – and the person will not be able to practise as a psychologist.)

By far the largest group of occupational psychologists are in government service, with a particular emphasis on aspects of employment and training. Occupational psychologists also work in research and advisory units, which might be government or privately funded. There are also opportunities in industry and commerce, although the organization is likely to be a major employer with many staff, before it chooses to set up its own psychology group. Smaller employers are likely to approach advisory services or individual consultants.

Research

There will always be some opportunities for employment in psychological research, either in educational establishments or in special research units. The most likely path to research is by preparing, over a period of at least three years, for a doctoral qualification. This involves the development of a piece of personal research, which is then submitted in a thesis and examined by a leading expert in the field.

Clearly, an excellent record at undergraduate level is an essential prerequisite, and the few grants available from the research councils, set aside for postgraduate research training, are awarded only to exceptional students. It is also possible to obtain work as a postgraduate research assistant, associated with a short-term research project, and to study for a PhD at the same time, either basing your thesis upon the work which has been funded as part of the project, or on separate work. Some of the government-funded research units are awarded special grants for graduates, to enable them to prepare for a higher degree.

While there will always be opportunities for research, the availability of research funds in all disciplines depends very much on the current state of the economy at large and the government's sense of priorities. I believe it should be possible for an exceptional student with a strong commitment to psychological research to obtain some means of preparing for a doctorate. There should be opportunities to obtain teaching posts in universities, polytechnics and institutes of further education in the next decade. The average age of present teaching staff is quite high and many will be contemplating retirement. At the same time psychology is seen as an essential component for many, non-psychological, professional training courses, such as physiotherapy or speech therapy. Unless you are particularly brilliant as a researcher, it may not be advisable to think in terms of a career purely in research; the most likely way in which you can spend time doing research and have a secure future, is in conjunction with a teaching post.

Psychology and the law

Scientists work in the prison service in a variety of capacities and include researchers, statisticians, occupational, and clinical psychologists. Many prison psychologists have undergone training in clinical psychology. Some have moved into administration within the prison service. Work may take place in ordinary prisons, special establishments, centres for young offenders or psychiatric prisons. Work can include counselling, therapy, training in social skills, assessments for the courts and probation service, staff training, and prison organization. Prison psychologists have made a particular contribution in helping other prison staff to work effectively in the very difficult conditions which can prevail in prison life.

During the first two years of employment there is a programme of supervision and opportunity to experience a variety of functions and environments. Special training courses and qualifications have been introduced recently. Prison psychologists have been very active in research and have made many contributions to our understanding of criminal and delinquent behaviour. A developing practitioner and research area is in relation to police work and legal processes. Psychologists are now training police in dealing with difficult situations, such as riots, hostage taking, domestic incidents, aggressive assaults, and breaking bad news. In the courts psychologists have been concerned with identity parade evidence, child witnesses and the behaviour of juries.

Teaching in schools and colleges

GCSE, A- and AS-Level psychology have become very popular. If this trend continues, then there will be opportunities for teaching posts in colleges of further education and schools. Psychology is taught to a variety of professional groups (see Chapter 2). It should be remembered that several years' experience in teaching in schools could be the first step in preparing for a career in educational psychology. A psychology graduate can therefore gain appropriate teaching experience by teaching psychology itself.

Other forms of employment

In Chapter 3, I argued that psychologists were good problem-solvers and excellent potential employees. Thus psychology offers something special as a degree education, even if one does not wish to pursue a career in psychology itself. Psychologists have a good chance of employment in careers with an emphasis on dealing with people (such as social work, careers guidance, the probation service, teaching, nursing). They also enter personnel work and general management training in commerce and industry. Between 1975 and 1985 the employment pattern for psychology graduates was as follows: public service 42 per cent; education 9 per cent; industry 14 per cent; commerce 23 per cent; other occupations 12 per cent. Such figures are not wholly reliable, but the proportions are probably a fair reflection of opportunities, given the prevailing fluctuations in the availability of work. Some new graduates choose to have a period away from paid work or study, acting as volunteer workers or travelling, as a means of broadening their views and experiences.

Community psychology and health psychology

These new areas of professional activity are placed together because they are growth areas. While opportunities at present are few, it is clear that we are on the brink of an expansion.

Community psychologists work largely in contexts we would associate with the social services and general medical practice. They may be concerned with community problems such as vandalism, squatting, violence at sports events, and provision for the socially deprived, but they are most likely to be working in social services in relation to special homes and in general service planning. Those who work in general medical practice are likely to be clinical psychologists with a strong commitment to community work, setting up programmes for smoking–cessation, sex education and therapy, drug abuse and other health-related problems. Given that some estimated 70 per cent of attendances at a general practitioner's surgery are seen to be psychologically related, many doctors now consider that there is a need for the employment of clinical psychologists within general practice. It is difficult to predict how much expansion there will be or at what speed.

As explained in Chapter 2, health psychology can be seen as a psychological sub-speciality of behavioural medicine. Psychologists may work in general hospitals, or in academic medical institutions. Social psychologists, with their expertise in changing attitudes and using social contexts to influence our behaviour, may also be involved. Such work would include smoking–cessation, controlling dietary behaviour, research and guidance on doctor–patient interaction, studies of psychological aspects of stress (including heart disease and cancer), and the application of psychological knowledge and research methodology to medical problems. Very recently several postgraduate courses in health psychology have been established. At the time of writing, however, there is no formally recognized profession called 'health psychology'.

Counselling

Counsellors spend a great deal of time listening to people. They encourage people to talk about themselves, their relationships and their feelings. When a person is distressed they can find it hard to confront painful aspects of their lives. Counsellors are skilled in helping people to face up to personal problems. While psychiatrists and clinical psychologists often describe those whom they help as *patients*, counsellors often make the point of using the word *clients*. There are several implications in this terminology. First, it emphasizes that the relationship is one of equality; the counsellor offers professional help, but not as a specialist with superior knowledge or special expertise. Another aspect of the equality of counsellor and client is the counsellor's willingness to express their own feelings, rather than hide behind a professional white coat, actual or metaphorical. Secondly, counsellors emphasize the person as a person and not as someone suffering from an illness. The person's own experiences and feelings are considered to be very important. They are seen to have within themselves the capacity to change their own lives; medication or special psychological treatments are not seen as particularly helpful. Thirdly, the counsellor sees himself or herself as a helper and facilitator; having helped the person to express their feelings and concerns, they then help them to acquire the means of supporting themselves emotionally and creating new conditions for living. Clients can be couples (as in marriage guidance), younger people with emotional problems, people who have suffered bereavement, groups such as nurses who have emotionally stressful jobs, patients in a hospice, and many other groups.

Most counsellors enter formal training after a period of work in some other field (social work, teaching, health visiting, psychiatry) and it is usual for courses to require a counsellor to have received personal counselling and to be supervised in their own work by an experienced counsellor.

Ethical issues

Because psychologists work and conduct research with people, there are special ethical responsibilities which must apply to their relationship with clients, patients, and experimental subjects. For example, *confidentiality* is of great importance: the client must feel able to speak freely, and the experimental subject must know that what is done in the laboratory may well appear as a set of numbers in a statistical table, but will be anonymous.

Another problem is that of *consent*; to give voluntary consent one needs to know what is involved in a procedure and to be able to make a free choice as to whether to undergo the procedure or not. Such a principle is not easy to apply with a patient who is mentally handicapped, or in a state of such anxiety and distress that balanced judgements cannot be made. Psychologists working as therapists will give clients the opportunity to withdraw from therapy if they change their mind about it after it has begun.

Such procedures (gaining consent, maintaining confidentiality) are consistent with a view of people as free agents with their own value systems, whose personal choice and history is a private matter. Difficulties can arise because psychologists are seen as experts, but there is nothing in that expertise which can enable them to tell other people how they should live; the aim is to help people to make their own choices. A psychologist may also have problems about identifying who the client is; for example, in the health and prison services, information does not belong to the individual but to the administrative body concerned. Thus, information given by a prisoner is not subject to the confidentiality principle; this can create conflict. The psychologist can be torn between a sense of personal loyalty to the individual prisoner, and a sense of duty to his or her employer, the prison service. Unlike the priest whose confessional has special protection, the psychologist in some circumstances cannot, strictly speaking, withhold valuable information, whatever its source.

As an undergraduate student you will need to respect the subjects of any experiment you conduct. If any proposed procedure seems potentially distressing, hazardous or deceptive, then you will need to consult with fellow students and your tutors, to decide if the purpose of the experiment justifies the procedure. There has been a recent shift in conventional language used to describe experimental subjects. Many psychology researchers now use the term 'participant' rather than 'subject'. The shift in language reflects a shift in attitudes.

Some students are distressed by the use of animals in experiments, and psychologists do disagree as to whether animal research is either justifiable in ethical terms or relevant to the explanation of human behaviour. There is no doubt that much of our knowledge of the functioning of the nervous system simply could not exist without animal research, since a high proportion of the research procedures could not conceivably be applied to human subjects. Animal researchers have made contributions in a variety of important fields of research, in relation to natural behaviour in the wild, learning, perception, anxiety and fear, the effects of reward and punishment, psychosomatic disease, and mechanisms underlying hunger and thirst. This is not the place to engage in a debate about the use of animals in psychological research. However, as an undergraduate you are unlikely to be allowed to do much work with animals, and staff will always accept that you are free to refuse to do so.

The British Psychological Society

The BPS has over 14,000 members and is the only scientific and professional society for psychologists in the UK incorporated by Royal Charter. It undertakes a wide range of functions, including the accreditation of postgraduate training courses, the organization of conferences, submitting psychological evidence to public bodies including government, and publishing scientific journals and books. The Society is organized into Sections and professional Divisions which have responsibility for vetting courses in clinical, educational, occupational and criminological and legal psychology. Since 1987 the Society has been authorized under the terms of its Royal Charter of incorporation to maintain a Register of Chartered Psychologists. Entry on the Register is restricted to members of the Society who have applied for registration and who have the necessary postgraduate qualifications or experience to have reached a standard sufficient for professional practice in psychology without supervision.

Students may join the Society at very reduced rates and purchase journals and books at discount. They will also receive the monthly magazine of the Society, *The Psychologist* and the *Appointments Memorandum*, both of which tell you a great deal about what is happening in British psychology and what career opportunities are open to you. If you attend one of the Society's conferences you are sure to meet and chat with some very famous psychologists, whose work you have read about in books. This gives a strong authentic flavour to your undergraduate work. The address of the Society is given on page iv at the front of this book.

5

Putting Theory into Practice: Applying Psychology to Yourself

The word 'theory' has been mentioned many times, and I have tried to give a picture of what a theory might look like. But I have written much more about hypotheses, hypothesis testing, the experiment, and the analysis and reporting of empirical data than I have about individual theories in psychology. I now mention some of the most influential views of what makes people tick, or theories about exactly what goes wrong with people when they fail to cope with life's problems. I have also written about applied psychology, its scientific basis and how professional psychologists are trained, but without offering worked examples of individual case-histories or successful interventions.

To avoid problems of confidentiality or consent I am going to invite you to consider a problem most of us have had at some time or another, the difficulty of getting down to work and of getting things done on time. If the problem applies to you, you can then be your own client and work as your own applied psychologist. This problem applies not only to homework at school, or to painting a room in your house that really does look shabby, or to tidying your living space, or filling in your income tax form, but to study at undergraduate level. I know few students who do not complain that they are not working hard enough, or that they are working so hard they never get things done, or that they do not know how they will cope.

A frequent conversation in my office can go like this: 'What do you think is wrong then?' 'I'm just lazy.' 'What does that mean?' 'I just can't get down to my work.' 'If lazy means that then it doesn't really explain anything.' 'You mean it's circular?' 'Good, you're beginning to think about it.' 'Oh, dear (deep groan of despair).' 'Anyway, I bet you won't find the word lazy in any psychology textbook.'

I am going to examine the problem of not being able to work from the point of view of several theories or approaches in psychology: general systems theory; motivation hierarchy, achievement motivation, job satisfaction–dissatisfaction; intelligence, aptitudes and interests; sensation seeking, and extraversion; intra-psychic conflict; anxiety and ego-defensiveness; locus of control and attribution theory; depression, learned helplessness and self-esteem; family systems theory; behavioural analysis; empathy, genuineness, and warmth. This sample of approaches should be sufficient to show how a theory works in an applied context. Each approach is associated with many volumes of scholarship and research and it will be difficult to do justice to any, in one or two paragraphs, and I have joined together things which other people might not. But a good challenge for a psychologist is to be able to say what you have to say in a few words. I must emphasize that this is not a textbook; if it were a formal psychology textbook, then I would cite authoritative references to support every claim I make.

Each example is presented in the way a psychologist or counsellor might wish to interpret what the client says. You can be an applied psychologist by acting as both client and counsellor. You can test whether the particular explanation fits your own case.

General systems theory

This is a theoretical approach borrowed from engineering and biology, and the main concepts are simple. It views the person as a system made up of sub-systems, all of which interact with each other. So a person's physiology, behaviour and subjective world are sub-systems. The whole is seen as greater than the parts, and when sub-systems interact consequences 'emerge' which would not occur if you looked at one of them alone. Such emergent properties make it hard to predict how a person will behave when examining only one or two aspects of their lives. If I were to adopt this approach in the present case, I would want to know about the person's health, eating habits, exercise, living habits, friendships, indeed any sub-system which might affect performance.

The approach does not lead to specific recommendations, but it does remind us that people are complex, and we should not rush to a simple-minded explanation. It would lead the psychologist to ensure that the person had no medical problem and to ask about their lifestyle, before seeking psychological explanations. The individual's intelligence might be high but their social world or health deficient; in combination, the outcome is poor performance. The approach also reminds you that the counselling context is a system too, combining the client, the counsellor and the interaction between them. Things can happen in such situations which do not happen elsewhere, and the client can say things (emergent properties) which do not happen elsewhere. The skilled counsellor will use this systems property wisely.

Motivation hierarchy, job satisfaction–dissatisfaction, and achievement motivation

Motivation, as the name implies, is about the things which drive or impel us to action, and sustain our activities. One theory states that we have a hierarchy of needs, each of the lowest needs on the hierarchy having to be satisfied in turn, before we can move on to higher needs. Thus physical needs essential for bodily survival come first, then the security of knowing physical needs will be satisfied in future, and so on, through social needs, self-esteem, and the highest need, self-actualization. This could lead us to ask the same questions as in general systems approaches, but the needs would be organized in a particular order, starting at the bottom of the hierarchy. It may be that the student has financial worries, which so undermine security needs that he or she cannot move on to the academic work which gives self-esteem and the approval of peers and teachers.

Job satisfaction theory is an extension of the hierarchy approach but in the context of working life. It treats the lower needs as 'hygiene' needs, claiming that if these needs (hunger, thirst, salary, social contacts) are met one is merely *not* dissatisfied; only higher needs, such as the opportunity to exercise skill and responsibility (motivators) lead to satisfaction. We could ask our student whether the subject he or she is studying really does offer a satisfying challenge. If not, according to the theory, no amount of cash or security will help to get a person involved with their studies.

Achievement motivation theory places the origins of our desire to achieve and excel in our early relationships with our parents and the ways in which we were rewarded in childhood. The mother of the high-achieving adult is claimed to be affectionate but to link the giving of attention to school and sports achievements, encouraging and rewarding independence and autonomy. According to the theory, a child brought up like that will never need to say he or she cannot work, since their motivation to achieve has a long history. Even away from home, the individual's sense of autonomy should stand them in good stead. Nevertheless the theory does lead us to ask our student how he or she has been rewarded (or even punished) for working or not working in the past. We could revive some past reward systems.

The achievement motivation approach is a developmental approach because it focuses on the individual's past history. Some interesting work in achievement motivation theory shows that people with strong and weak drives to achieve make different estimates of what they can achieve and their chances of success. So the drive not only impels the person but sets the goals also. A person may be capable of high achievement but be held back through lack of confidence. In such cases a counsellor would guide the client into exploring their own motives and value systems. It might be appropriate to consider the history of a person's motives and the forces which sustain them. For example, the origins of our self-esteem may lie in early childhood and events which occurred in the intimate context of family life. The related concept of self-esteem is considered below.

Intelligence, aptitudes and interests

Here we refer to the psychological testing tradition and the notion that people have inborn traits or psychological characteristics which are permanent aspects of their make-up and which determine their behaviour. It is unlikely that some one reading for a psychology degree has insufficient intellect to cope with the course, because the hurdles leading to entry are so high. But I have warned that psychology can be a shock to someone who finds scientific work and statistical methods unsuited to their particular abilities or interests. I have had students who have had problems with psychology, but have then moved on to other subjects which seem to make demands on talents which the student had but could not deploy on the courses they were failing in. This approach is dependent on identifying aspects of the person incompatible with the demands imposed by the environment. The intervention takes the form of trying to match the person to the job, and vice versa. Quite often a person may not appreciate their own particular talents or may persist in trying to achieve things for which they are not well suited. Psychometric and aptitude tests may be used to identify the individual's talents and strengths, so that they can be used to the best advantage. For example, it would not be sensible for someone to start a career in computer programming if a test of computer aptitude revealed a lack of appropriate skills.

Sensation-seeking and extraversion

This is also a trait approach. Like achievement motivation it is concerned with drives rather than abilities, like intelligence; but, as with intelligence, it believes that the traits reflect inbuilt characteristics. The sensation–seeker cannot get down to work because it does not provide enough sensation; academic work involves sitting down and attending for long periods, and can become monotonous, particularly if you have a need to be active and do things, go out and meet people. The extravert is said to be someone who prefers activity, people, a changing environment, and variety. One study of extraverts', behaviour in libraries showed that they are more likely than introverts to sit near people or opposite people, even when there is plenty of room! Again, extreme extraversion is not compatible with the hard work which leads to examination success. Extraverts may well choose occupations more suited to their temperament, and someone offering vocational guidance would suggest jobs which involve plenty of activity, opportunities to meet people, and work which offers variety and challenge and does not impose a repetitive routine.

Intra-psychic conflict, anxiety, and ego-defensiveness

Psychoanalytic theory, first developed by Sigmund Freud, placed a lot of our motivations within the unconscious, and many of our failures to cope with life's pressures are seen to be a result of deep and unconscious conflict. The ego has the job of balancing the needs of the id (instinct and desire), with the high ideals, foreboding and disapproval of the superego (the conscience) in the context of environmental reality, i.e. what the world can offer. Unresolved conflict creates anxiety, which itself can be disruptive of normal functioning.

One of the ways the ego copes is to construct *defences* to protect our psychological health. For example, we may feel guilty about not working, so we say 'the course isn't worth doing' (rationalization), or 'the teachers are awful' (projection), or 'I'm not really worried' (denial), or 'everything is fantastic, OK, really good' (repression), or 'it was so much nicer 10 years ago when I was home with my parents' (regression). You may recognize this sort of strategy in yourself or others.

A psychoanalyst will not tackle personal problems head on, and the process of psychoanalysis is lengthy, because it involves getting at material in the unconscious which is protected by defences. I should say here that psychoanalysis is regarded by many psychologists as being little more than superstition, based on insecure evidence, and not much help to people with problems. Unfortunately, I myself have a sneaking feeling that there is more to psychoanalysis than meets many a psychologist's eye; some departments in the UK do offer optional courses in psychoanalysis, but they are rare. It is certainly true that psychoanalysis, a special approach to therapy, involving many years of specialist training (usually involving training in medicine and psychiatry) is *not* psychology and should not be confused with it.

Locus of control and attribution theory

So far we have talked of drives, unconscious conflicts, and inborn traits. The theories now under discussion focus more on cognitive processes, the ways in which we interpret our world. Locus of control is seen both as a personality characteristic and a style of thinking. The person with an external locus believes we are at the mercy of fate and uncontrollable outside influences; this means that, given we have no control over events, it is not really worth trying to control them. The person with an internal locus sees themself as being in charge of their own life and of controlling what goes on in their world. The student who cannot work may be someone who feels that work will not bring positive consequences and that effort is pointless.

Attribution theory is also about our explanations of events. Attribution can relate to self or others, or to permanent or shortlived circumstances. For example, if someone is rude to you at a party you could say: 'I'm horrible, no wonder no one likes me (self, permanent)', or 'I wasn't at my best that evening (self, temporary)', or 'That's one of the most unpleasant people I've ever met (other, permanent)', or, finally, 'poor chap had just had a row with his boss (other, temporary)'. A person who tends to attribute all bad things to their own permanent characteristics is likely to be very depressed and hopeless. It is particularly bad if one has a global view of one's incompetence – that you are lousy at *everything* you do. Attributing nasty events to other people can get you over the immediate stress, but it might not be a very good strategy for the future, because you could be misleading yourself (as with defence mechanisms, it is a projection in some circumstances). The counsellor would work through the person's interpretations of their own past. They may also ask the person to keep a diary, noting down every occasion when they view their own behaviour in a negative way. This helps the person to appreciate that they have an automatic tendency to colour their own actions in a negative light. Such a recognition is the first step in changing your attitude to yourself. I am unfortunate in attributing all good things which happen to my own efforts, and all bad things to other people's incompetence or villainy. Am I alone?

Depression, learned helplessness and self-esteem

Sometimes, failure to get down to work, listlessness, poor appetite, loss of sleep, and lack of any sense of pleasure in life can be signs of depression. Given the incidence of psychological disorders in the population I am not surprised that our sample of students includes people with severe (if only temporary) psychological problems. I would certainly not seek to deal with them myself, merely on a counselling basis (I am not a clinical psychologist and I do not have a clinical responsibility). I would therefore take the student to the student health service, assuming that he or she agreed to come.

Learned helplessness is a psychological explanation of depressive states and is associated with attribution theory. The depressed person has learned that no matter what they do their position is helpless. There is some evidence, for example, that people liable to depression may have lost a parent in childhood (when they could do little to comfort themselves or change their world), have had previous depressive bouts, and have difficult life circumstances (physical illness, low income, poor housing, no friends). Such people suffer from a loss of self–esteem because they cannot see themselves as powerful or effective. The same is true of the elderly, who can suffer from loss of hope, particularly when deprived of a sense of self–worth if they have few resources, have lost a lifelong companion or are placed in an unfriendly institutional environment, and believe they are merely waiting to die. Of course, most people who have suffered loss do not succumb to depression, but learned helplessness theory points to the notion of people at risk. In this case, then, failure to get down to work is just part of a general state; in the case of our extraverted student, there was plenty of energy around, but it was directed in the wrong places. Depression is known to have physical, behavioural, and subjective content, and theories of depression reflect this (there are biochemical, developmental, learning, intra–psychic and cognitive theories). However, there is growing evidence that cognitive therapy, getting the person to change the ways they think about the world, themselves and the future, is equally or more effective in treating depression than anti-depressant drugs. One reason for this is that learning to think differently about yourself makes you an active agent in your treatment and gives you a psychological toolkit to deal with your own present and future problems.

Family systems theory

Family systems theory is another form of general systems theory but in the family context. If someone becomes a patient the notion is that he or she is part of a system and it might be misleading to identify them as the real patient. The family as a whole is a patient. For example, a child who wets the bed, or throws tantrums, or starts fires, or refuses to go to school, may be reflecting conflict elsewhere in the family (say major emotional and communication problems between the child's parents). The child's 'illness' serves as a distraction or a means of defence in the psychoanalytic sense; it unites parents and helps them avoid confronting their own conflict. Thus therapists treat the whole family because focusing on the child will not change the real problem.

Quite often, my students, who are newly away from home, do bring their family problems with them to the university without realizing it. I am not a therapist, nor of course, is the family present, but quite often students can discover that they came to talk about a work problem but then seem to be spending most of their time talking about problems miles away, at home. Again, we see the work problem is just a symptom of other, unresolved issues. Families go through a life cycle in which it takes time to adjust to new circumstances. For example, rules which work for a compliant eight year old are not appropriate for a resentful adolescent. Later, the student leaving home may create a gap in the parents' lives. Parents who have devoted many years to their children can suffer a severe sense of loss when they leave home to study. It can take time for all parties involved to adjust to new circumstances. The aim of family therapy is to change the family as an organization. This involves establishing channels of communication, clarifying the roles of each family member, enabling each person to express negative feelings such as resentment and frustration and guiding family members into swapping good feelings for bad.

The behavioural approach

I favour this approach, because I find it the most manageable and the most amenable to a scientific evaluation. Essentially it sees the person's world in terms of behaviour, circumstances, and rewards and punishments. First I would ask the student to describe in detail exactly what happens when they try to study but fail; this is the first level of description. We can then discuss what should happen, again in some detail (sitting down, often in a familiar position, having the materials ready, telling friends one is not free, setting realistic goals, dividing the work up into manageable units, not trying to work when one is tired, being active rather than passive while working). We can then talk about what is rewarding (cup of coffee, playing the guitar, going to the pub, seeing one's friends) and try to see how such rewards can be tied in to sensible working patterns. Thus, read a page, check if you understand it, go over it, feel good (reward), do some more, don't spend hours looking at something you can't understand (punishment), start with easier things (reward), work for reasonable periods then stop for some guitar practice (reward), after a successful bout go to the pub (good reward), meet your friends and tell them you have done some work, win their approval (reward) . . . and so on. One tries to get control over the circumstances, shapes the behaviour to realistic goals, and rewards correct behaviour, avoiding opportunities for punishment and feelings of gloom and apathy.

Note that this approach deals with the here and now and does not imply inner conflicts or inadequate personality characteristics. It depends on objective description and control. It can be evaluated because, having divided the work into units, one can keep a record of the degree of improvement. One can even suggest going back to the old ways, as a control, just to see if the old bad habits return. Such a behavioural approach has proved useful in many contexts. It is not always appropriate, but I find it does appeal to students because it depends so much on the psychological knowledge they have acquired about learning and the mechanisms of reward. It also shifts them out of the cul-de-sac of some trait and psychoanalytic theories, which offer little hope of immediate practical assistance. It has the advantage of being supervised by the person themself, thus offering a sense of self-control, and it soon gives results which are apparent. Here I can safely leave the student to be their own applied psychologist.

Empathy, genuineness and warmth

This is about the therapist's style or even technical approach, and not about the causes of a problem of adjustment. It is claimed, by humanistic psychologists (psychologists who consider *human* experience and subjective reality to be of crucial importance), that certain sorts of therapist or counsellor are more effective than others, and that counsellors can be trained to behave in certain ways. Empathy means sharing the client's feelings and acknowledging such feelings are possible in yourself, genuineness means that you do not set yourself apart from the client or hide behind a professional mask, and warmth means that you accept the client as a person, warts and all. This contrasts with the cartoon sketch of the therapist sitting behind the client with a notebook, the client not seeing the therapist's face but looking at the ceiling; thus the therapist appears as an authoritative and powerful figure, very much in command of the encounter.

Scientifically controlled studies with detailed observations of both therapist and client behaviour indicate that the empathy, genuineness and warmth approach is effective, particularly for young people. The notion is that the counsellor gives an unqualified commitment to the client, accepting the client in every way. When I first went to university I could not approach my tutors for help; their role was one of *in loco parentis* (a sort of substitute Victorian parent) and the rules which governed our lives were strict and authoritarian. I believe the modern tutor to be typically more sympathetic and understanding, not imposing their own value systems on a reluctant student. The model of the person has shifted over time, from someone to be controlled by others, to someone who is expected to exercise personal control and accept personal responsibility.

A conclusion

You should look back over these different theories and see how they offer different interpretations of a common problem. Often they seem to overlap with each other. In some cases (psychoanalysis versus behavioural approaches) they come into direct conflict with each other, for one deals with a hidden, mysterious and unconscious hidden world, while the other depends on observable behaviour and measurable environmental contingencies. The different theories represent different approaches in psychology: systems, medical, behavioural, cognitive, individual differences, family, intrapsychic, developmental and humanistic. Each of them in their own way emphasizes or de-emphasizes the *biological, learning, social* and *individual differences* influences on human *behaviour* and *experience*. In coming to the end of this book we seem to have returned, full circle, to where we started for these are the key constituents of the human condition.

I hope that I have managed to give you a sense of the challenge, fun and pleasure which the study of psychology can bring. In the Appendices which follow you will find information not only about books which can be used to follow up on the issues raised in this volume, but about career paths and opportunities in psychology.

If we ever meet I hope you will tell me what you think about this book. If you have any strong views about it, why not write to me at Southampton University?

Acknowledgement

I could not have hoped for more tolerance, kindness and practical help than I received from Cassy Spearing and Clare Skidmore. Many thanks.

APPENDIX A

Useful books about psychology and careers in psychology

General introduction to the nature of psychology
COLMAN, A.M. (1988) *What is Psychology? The inside story*. London: Hutchinson.
COLMAN, A.M. (1987) *Facts, Fallacies and Frauds in Psychology*. London: Hutchinson.

Especially written for adult education students
BERRYMAN, J., HARGREAVES, D., HOWELLS, K. and HOLLIN, C. (1987) *Psychology and You: An informal introduction*. Leicester: BPS Books & Routledge.

GCSE psychology
HAYES, N. (1988) *A First Course in Psychology*, 2nd ed. London: Harrap.
SYLVA, K. and LUNT, I. (1982) *Child Development: A first course*. Oxford: Blackwell.

A-Level and AS-Level
GROSS, R.D. (1987) *Psychology: The science of mind and behaviour*. London: Edward Arnold.

Where to study psychology
COMMITTEE OF DIRECTORS OF POLYTECHNICS SECRETARIAT (1989) *Polytechnic Courses Handbook*. London: Committee of Directors of Polytechnics Secretariat.
COMMITTEE OF VICE-CHANCELLORS AND PRINCIPALS (1989) *University Choice*. London: Sheed & Ward.
MOHINDRA, N. (1989) *Degree Course Guide 1989/1990: Psychology in UK universities, polytechnics and colleges*. Cambridge: Hobsons.
STANDING CONFERENCE OF PRINCIPALS (1989) *Guide to Institutes and Colleges of Higher Education*. Ormskirk: Standing Conference of Principals.

To help you decide if psychology is for you
BALL, B. (1989) *Manage Your Own Career: A self-help guide to career planning*. Leicester: BPS Books & Kogan Page.
HIGGINS, L.T. (1988) *Career Choices in Psychology: A guide to graduate opportunities*. Leicester: BPS Books.
HIGGINS, L.T. (1989) *How About Psychology?* Leicester: BPS Books.

NEWSTEAD, S., MILLER, M. and FARMER, E. (1989) *Putting Psychology to Work.* Leicester: BPS Books.

Degree-level introductory texts
ATKINSON, R.L., ATKINSON, R.C. and HILGARD, E.R. (1987) *Introduction to Psychology,* 9th ed. New York: Harcourt, Brace, Jovanovich.
GLEITMAN, H. (1986) *Psychology,* 2nd ed. New York: Norton.

Useful guides once you are a psychology student
AMERICAN PSYCHOLOGICAL ASSOCIATION (1982) *Ethical Principles in the Conduct of Research with Human Participants.* Washington: American Psychological Association.
HARRIS, P. (1986) *Designing and Reporting Experiments.* Milton Keynes: Open University Press.
REED, J.G. and BAXTER, P.M. (1983) *Library Use: A handbook for psychology.* Washington: American Psychological Association.
STERNBERG, R.J. (1988) *The Psychologist's Companion: A guide to scientific writing for students and researchers.* New York: Cambridge University Press and BPS Books.

Applied psychology
EDWARDS, H. (1987) *Psychological Problems: Who can help?* Leicester: BPS Books.
GALE, A. and CHAPMAN, A.J. (Eds) (1984) *Psychology and Social Problems: An introduction to applied psychology.* Chichester: Wiley.
WARR, P. (Ed) (1987) *Psychology at Work,* 3rd ed. Harmondsworth: Penguin.

Examples of research exercises in psychology
BENJAMIN, L.T. and LOWMAN, K.D. (Eds) (1983) *Activities Handbook for the Teaching of Psychology.* Washington: American Psychological Association.
BREAKWELL, G.M., FOOT, H. and GILMOUR, R. (1988) *Doing Social Psychology: Laboratory and field exercises.* New York: Cambridge University Press and BPS Books.

Teaching psychology
CLARK, D. and DAVIES, G. (1988) *Handbook for Psychology Teachers.* Leicester: Association for the Teaching of Psychology (c/o The BPS).
RADFORD, J. and Rose, D. (1989) *A Liberal Science.* Milton Keynes: Open University.

Up-to-date view of psychology in the UK
The Psychologist (published monthly). Leicester: The BPS.

Postgraduate courses in psychology
ASSOCIATION OF HEADS OF DEPARTMENTS OF PSYCHOLOGY (1989) *Compendium of UK Postgraduate Courses in Psychology.* Guildford: Department of Psychology, University of Surrey.
THE BPS (1987) *Postgraduate Qualifications and Courses in Psychology.* Leicester: The BPS.

APPENDIX B

Key contents of undergraduate courses

Biological bases of behaviour

+ Evolution
+ Human genetics (transmission of characteristics across generations and interaction of inherited traits with the environment)
+ Ethology, communication and social behaviour in animals (usually in natural settings)
+ Principles of development (biological factors in the development of the individual)
+ The cell, the neurone, neuronal transmission (how messages are passed between basic nervous system elements)
+ Anatomy and physiology of the nervous system (key structures and systems)
+ Biochemistry and electrophysiology of the nervous system (chemical and electrical aspects of many features of behaviour)
+ Central nervous system (higher centres) and autonomic nervous system (automatic brain control of the heart and other internal organs)
+ Hormones (internal chemical messengers)
+ The cerebral hemispheres (how different sides of the brain are specialized)
+ Neuropsychology (including brain mechanisms underlying language and speech and the effects of damage to the brain upon psychological functioning)
+ The senses (for example, vision, hearing, taste)
+ Perception (how sensory information is processed to give experience of objects and people)
+ Pain (physiological and psychological factors)
+ Transmission of information within the nervous system (coding, storage and integration of information)
+ The effects of drugs (including addiction and dependence)
+ Memory, storage, consolidation and retrieval (electrical and chemical aspects of memory)
+ Physiological bases of motivation (brain centres underlying drives)
+ Mechanisms underlying hunger, thirst, sex, temperature regulation
+ The expression of emotion (through feelings, facial expression, bodily activity)
+ Motor movement (aspects of posture, balance and complex skills)
+ Arousal (alertness), consciousness and sleep (including dreaming and the functions of sleep)

Learning and thinking

+ Animal learning (in the wild and in the laboratory)
+ Classical conditioning (simple associative learning first studied by Pavlov)
+ Instrumental or operant learning (more complex learning studied by Skinner)
+ Reward and punishment (are they

beneficial for learning?)
+ Fear and avoidance
+ Learning theories
+ Instincts and early learning
+ Cognitive learning (higher learning processes by which we learn to represent the world and understand it)
+ Short-term (immediate) and long-term memory
+ Semantic memory (recall of general knowledge independent of context in which learned)
+ Perception and the representation of knowledge
+ Metamemory (awareness of one's own memory processes)
+ Reading
+ Attention
+ Concept formation
+ Problem solving
+ Heuristics (rules people use to solve problems)
+ Artificial intelligence (computer modelling of human intellectual processes)
+ Language acquisition
+ Psycholinguistics (how we understand and use language)
+ Skills and errors (highly complex routines and how we make mistakes)

Social psychology

+ Attachment and early social relationships (relationship between child and family members)
+ Self and others (how we learn to have a sense of being a separate individual)
+ Social cognition (our understanding of social relationships)
+ Social representations (cultural and group meanings attached to important concepts such as gender, work, money)
+ Impression formation (how we see others)
+ Friendship
+ Frustration and aggression

+ Attitudes, attitude formation and attitude change
+ Stereotypes and prejudice
+ Social influence
+ Social facilitation (the influence of the presence of other people on our behaviour)
+ Obedience and compliance
+ Attribution theory (our explanations of how and why things happen)
+ Equity theory (human relations seen as an 'economic' exchange)
+ Social comparison theory (our tendency to compare ourselves with others)
+ Small groups
+ Crowds
+ Leadership
+ Decision making
+ Organizational behaviour
+ Institutional behaviour (how people behave in prisons and psychiatric institutions etc.)
+ Intergroup relations
+ Bargaining and negotiation
+ Social origins of gender differences

Individual differences

+ Psychoanalytic theory (Sigmund Freud and his followers and the notion of unconscious motives)
+ Social learning theory
+ Anxiety (and how it affects our behaviour)
+ Conscience (how we acquire a sense of right and wrong and our moral values)
+ Personal construct theory (how people's personal beliefs affect their behaviour and psychological health)
+ Trait theory (characteristics such as extraversion)
+ Lifespan approaches (the individual seen throughout the life cycle)
+ Ageing
+ Theories of self
+ Trait-situation interaction
+ Intelligence
+ Aptitudes

+ Creativity and genius
+ Gender differences in psychological functioning and how they arise
+ Psychometric measurement (principles of psychological testing)
+ Psychiatric disorders and their causes
+ Psychiatric diagnosis
+ Models of psychological disturbance
+ Schizophrenia and the psychoses (very serious mental illnesses)
+ The neuroses (disorders arising from anxiety)
+ Mental handicap
+ Stress
+ Depression
+ Personality disorders
+ Delinquency and crime
+ Psychotherapies (psychological treatment of mental illness)
+ Psychopharmacology (psychological effects of the use of drugs as treatments)
+ Stigma (society's reactions to the mentally ill person)
+ Gender differences in the incidence of psychiatric disorders
+ Animal models of mental illness

Applied psychology

+ Clinical psychology (treatment of psychological disorders)
+ Educational psychology (psychological work in schools and with children)
+ Occupational or industrial psychology
+ Community psychology
+ Behavioural medicine and health psychology
+ Forensic psychology (psychology and legal process and prison psychology)
+ Assessment, selection and training (vocational guidance, fitting the person and the job)
+ Organizational change agents
+ Counselling
+ Sports psychology
+ Evaluation of psychological interventions

Psychological method, design and statistics

+ Principles of measurement
+ The design of experiments
+ Controlling for unwanted influences
+ Probability and tests of statistical significance
+ Reliability
+ Randomization
+ Sources of error and their control
+ Analysis of variance
+ Correlation and regression
+ Ranking methods
+ Analysis of trends and time series
+ Observational sampling techniques
+ Interviewing
+ Survey methods and the design of questionnaires
+ Qualitative research techniques
+ Case studies and studies of single objects
+ Ethical issues in psychological research (including voluntary consent, privacy, confidentiality, briefing, work with animals)
+ Instrumentation
+ Computers in psychological experiments and computer programming.

APPENDIX C

A degree course guide to universities, polytechnics and colleges in the UK and Eire

---

An introduction to Tables A and B

Table A lists all the institutions in the United Kingdom and Eire which offer degree qualifications in psychology. For each department there is a list of the degree schemes available, how long each degree takes to complete, how many student places are available, the number of teaching staff, how much choice you have in selecting particular options or courses, how many hours of teaching there are each week, and how much of the final assessment is based on formal examinations (rather than course work).

Table B gives you the full address and phone number of each department, provides information about the key research interests of the department, and tells you whether they offer postgraduate courses (either in special areas of psychology, such as intelligence systems, or for professional qualifications, for example in clinical psychology).

Please note that not all the degrees shown in Table A are accepted as conferring the Graduate Basis for Registration with The British Psychological Society (which is necessary if you wish to become a Chartered Psychologist). You should ask the institution where you wish to study whether their degrees are recognized by the BPS. Always make sure you read their prospectus carefully for full details about the degrees offered before you fill in any application form.

The information given in Tables A and B was obtained from departments and was correct at the time of going to press. If any department has introduced major changes kindly write to the author and let him know. A list of the abbreviations used in both tables is given on page 121.

General notes for Table A

Course titles. Psychology degrees are taught in faculties of arts, social sciences, or science. The designation of BA or BSc is not a sure indication of the content of the degree, the main difference being entry qualifications and/or the auxiliary subjects studied. Universities in Scotland usually offer four-year degrees leading to an MA. Students study a wide range of subjects in the first year, and generally do not need to choose their main degree subject(s) until the end of the first year (or even the second year). In some cases, students with good A-Level results may be exempted from the first year. Quite often, permission to take psychology honours will depend on performance in the end of year examinations.

Combined honours degrees typically involve two main subjects, studied in parallel, with roughly equal time devoted to each throughout the degree course.

Ordinary or general degrees denote a lower level of qualification than an honours degree.

Special entry requirements are those particular to a psychology department and will be in addition to an institution's general entry requirements. Before making an application, be sure that you study the institution's prospectus very carefully; for example, science degrees in psychology may require passes in A-Level science subjects as a faculty requirement. Note also that at some institutions, selection of students is not carried out by the department of psychology itself but at a higher level of the organization (school or faculty). Most departments of psychology require a good pass (grade C or better) in GCSE Maths; equivalents to GCSE are often acceptable, particularly in the case of mature students.

Student numbers given are the number of final-year students in a typical year.

Staff numbers indicate the number of full-time teaching staff in the psychology department or psychology teaching group. Many departments also have part-time lecturers. (For combined honours courses, the staff teaching the associated subject have not been included in the total.)

Psychology options. This column indicates whether you have any choice regarding which psychology courses you take in each year. If a department offers a variety of degrees, the figures given here are for single honours psychology (BA and/or BSc).

Psychology contact hours per week shows how much time is spent each week in lecture theatres, seminars/tutorials and practical classes. If a department offers a variety of degrees, the figure given here is for single honours psychology (BA and/or BSc).

Percentage of each year's assessment attributed to formal exams shows how much of the assessment each year is allocated to formal examinations as opposed to course work. Note that this column does not indicate whether or not work in all years contributes to the final degree class; for most degree courses the final degree class is largely based on achievements in the second and final year.

General notes for Table B

Institution. To make an enquiry write to the Admissions Tutor at the address given.

Research areas. To compile this table departments were invited to give three key areas of research in which they were involved. Take the areas given as a rough guide to the research interests of the teaching staff.

As with the research areas listing, *postgraduate qualifications by courses in psychology* are given to provide you with a flavour of a department's interests and work and to indicate which professional group of psychology is represented within the department.

Table A

Title of course	No. of years	Special entry requirements	Student nos.	Staff nos.	Psychology options	Psychology contact hours per week Lectures	Seminars	Lab work	Percentage of each year's assessment attributed to formal exams
Aberdeen University									
BSc designated degree ☆	3	none	4	11	Ys 1-2: none; Y3: 3 from 6; Y4: 3 from 6	Y1 3 / Y2 4 / Y3 6 / Y4 5	0 / 1 / 4 / 4	2 / 2 / 4 / 4	Y1 100% / Y2 100% / Y3 no exams / Y4 85%
BSc Sing. Hons	4		12						
MA Sing. Hons	4		23						
MA Comb. Hons w. Philosophy	4		1						
BSc Comb. Hons w. Computing	4		0						
Aston University									
BSc Sing. Hons*	3	GCSE Maths	35	10	Ys 1-2: none; Y3: 4 from 6	Y1 7 / Y2 7 / Y3 8	2 / 2 / 1	8 / 8 / RP	Y1 64% / Y2 64% / Y3 20% / Y4 56%
BSc Comb. Hons w. 1 from poss. 6 subjects *	3								
Bath University									
BSc Comb. Hons w. Sociology**	4	GCSE Maths	12	4	Ys 1-4: none	Y1 5 / Y2 5 / Y3 PLACEMENT / Y4 8	2 / 2 / / 0	4 / 2 / / RP	Y1 50% / Y2 50% / Y3 no exams / Y4 35%
Queen's University of Belfast									
BA Sing. Hons	3	none	40	18	Ys 1-2: none; Y3: 6 from 12	Y1 3 / Y2 8 / Y3 9	0 / 1 / 2	2 / 3 / RP	Y1 67% / Y2 75% / Y3 40%
BSc Sing. Hons	3		25						
BSSc Sing. Hons	3		25						

Birmingham University

Course	A-levels	Requirements							
BSc Sing. Hons	3	⎫	45	18	Ys 1-2: none; Y3: 4 from 12	Y1 12 / Y2 12 / Y3 4	1 / 1 / 2	6 / 6 / RP	Y1 40% / Y2 40% / Y3 40%
BSc Comb. Hons w. Maths	3	⎬ GCSE Maths	6						
BSc Comb. Hons w. Sports & Exercise Science	3	⎭	6						

Bolton Institute of H.E.

Course	A-levels	Requirements							
BSc Sing. Hons ☆	3	(A-Level Maths, P. or a science preferred)	70	18	Y1: none; Y2: 1 from 4; Y3: 2 from 8	Y1 7 / Y2 4 / Y3 3	5 / 4 / 3	3 / 4 / RP	Y1 50% / Y2 50% / Y3 80%

Bristol University

Course	A-levels	Requirements							
BSc (SocSci) Sing. Hons	3	⎫	18	11	Ys 1-2: none; Y3: 5 from 9	Y1 3 / Y2 7 / Y3 5	⅓ / ½ / ½	3 / 5 / RP	Y1 92% / Y2 no exams / Y3 72%
BSc (SocSci) Comb. Hons w. Sociology	3	⎬ GCSE Maths	6						
Sociology	3	⎭	6						
BSc (SocSci) Comb. Hons w. Philosophy	3	⎫ GCSE Maths + 2 approved science A-levels	20						
BSc Sing. Hons	3	⎬	6						
BSc Comb. Hons w. Zoology		⎭							

Brunel University

Course	A-levels	Requirements							
BSc Sing. Hons **	4	⎫	25	8	Ys 1-2: none; Ys 3-4: 8 from 14	Y1 8 / Y2 6 / Y3 6 / Y4 6	4 / 3 / 3 / 3	3 / 3 / RP	Y1 69% (av.) / Y2 56% (av.) / Y3 54% (av.) / Y4 54% (av.)
BSc Comb. Hons w. Social Anthropology **	4	⎬ GCSE Maths/ internal test	9						
BSc Comb. Hons w. Sociology **	4		9						
BSc Comb. Hons in SocSci **	4	⎭	1-2						

Buckingham University

Course	A-levels	Requirements							
BA Joint Hons w. Biology, Business Studies or Computer Science	2	GCSE Maths	20	4	Y1: none; Y2: 5 from 7	Y1 3 / Y2 3	1½ / 1½	1-3 / 1-3	Y1 60% / Y2 60%

Title of course	No. of years	Special entry requirements	Student nos.	Staff nos.	Psychology options	Psychology contact hours per week			Percentage of each year's assessment attributed to formal exams
						Lectures	Seminars	Lab work	
Cambridge University									
BA Comb. Hons in Natural Sciences	3	initial selection by individual colleges; entry to P. course after Y2	48	15	Ys 1-2: none; Y3: represent 50% of course work	Y1 0 / Y2 3 / Y3 6	Y1 0 / Y2 1 / Y3 4	Y1 0 / Y2 4 / Y3 RP	Y1 no exams / Y2 100% / Y3 80%
Central London Polytechnic									
BSc Comb. Hons (Psychology Pathway)	3	1 science A-level	20	5	Ys 1-3: none	Y1 3¾ / Y2 2¾ / Y3 3	Y1 2¼ / Y2 6¼ / Y3 ¾	Y1 2½ / Y2 2¼ / Y3 7½	Y1 no exams / Y2 66% / Y3 66%
Chester College of H.E.									
BA Comb. Hons w. 1-2 of poss. 10 other subjects	3	GCSE Maths, Statistics or A-Level P.	30	4	Ys 1-3: none	Y1 2 / Y2 4 / Y3 4	Y1 1 / Y2 1 / Y3 2	Y1 2 / Y2 2 / Y3 0	Y1 50% / Y2 75% / Y3 75%
BSc Comb. Hons w. 1-2 of poss. 5 other subjects	3		5						
City of London Polytechnic									
BSc Sing. Hons P./P. in Practice	3	none	70	17	Y1: none; Ys 2-3: 9 from 19	Y1 4 / Y2 7 / Y3 6	Y1 2 / Y2 4 / Y3 4	Y1 2 / Y2 3 / Y3 RP	Y1 60% / Y2 80% / Y3 60%
BA/BSc Comb. Hons modular degree in Neuroscience or Organizational Behaviour or 1-2 of poss. 14 other subjects	3		80						
BSc Sing. Hons. Computing w. Human Factors	3		50						

City University

Course	Yrs	Entry requirements	No.		Assessment				
BSc Sing. Hons	3	GCSE Maths & Eng. Lang.	14	8	Y1: 3 from 5; Y2: none; Y3: 4 from 6	Y1 2 / Y2 10 / Y3 8	Y1 1 / Y2 1 / Y3 0	Y1 3 / Y2 3 / Y3 RP	Y1 80% / Y2 80% / Y3 64%
BSc Comb. Hons w. any combination of Sociology, Philosophy & Economics, Systems Science and Nursing	3		10						

Coventry Polytechnic

Course	Yrs	Entry requirements	No.		Assessment				
BA Comb. Hons in Applied SocSci ☆	3	none	70	5	Ys 1-3: none	Y1 5 / Y2 5 / Y3 5	Y1 5 / Y2 5 / Y3 5	Y1 2 / Y2 2 / Y3 2	Y1 75% / Y2 75% / Y3 75%

Crewe & Alsager College of H.E.

Course	Yrs	Entry requirements	No.		Assessment				
BSc Comb. Hons in Sport Science	3	1 science A-level & GCSE Maths & Eng. Lang. (GCSE Maths preferred)	36	5	Ys 1-3: none	Y1 5 / Y2 4½ / Y3 2¾	Y1 2½ / Y2 3 / Y3 3¾	Y1 6 / Y2 6 / Y3 2¾	Y1 50% / Y2 20% / Y3 20%
BA Hons in Independent Study	3		20						

Dundee University

Course	Yrs	Entry requirements	No.		Assessment				
MA Sing. Hons	4	none	25	13	Ys 1-2: none; Ys 3-4: 7 from 14	Y1 3 / Y2 3 / Y3 4 / Y4 5	Y1 0 / Y2 0 / Y3 1 / Y4 2	Y1 1-3 / Y2 1-3 / Y3 3 / Y4 RP	Y1 25% / Y2 66% / Y3 no exams / Y4 84%
BSc Sing. Hons	4	GCSE Maths	15						
MA/BSc Joint Hons w. 2 of poss. 11 other subjects	4	varies w. subject	10						
MA/BSc Comb. Hons w. 1 of poss. 11 other subjects									

Title of course	No. of years	Special entry requirements	Student nos.	Staff nos.	Psychology options	Psychology contact hours per week			Percentage of each year's assessment attributed to formal exams
						Lectures	Seminars	Lab work	
Durham University									
BA Sing. Hons	3		} 31	10	Ys 1-2: none; Y3: 3 from 9	Y1 3 Y2 7 Y3 7	1 1 1	3 3 3	Y1 70% Y2 73% Y3 42% (av.)
BSc Sing. Hons	3								
BA Comb. Hons w. Anthropology, Philosophy or Sociology	3	GCSE Maths							
BA Comb. Hons in SocSci	3		} 12						
BSc Comb. Hons in Natural Sciences	3								
Ealing College of H.E.									
BA Sing. Hons	3	none	75	8	Y1: none; Ys 2-3: 7 from 9	Y1 1 Y2 3 Y3 4	1 3 4	2 2 RP	Y1 50% Y2 70% Y3 70%
Polytechnic of East London									
BSc Sing. Hons	3	(GCSE Maths & Eng. Lang. preferred)	80 35 20	36	Y1: 2 from 5 Y2: 3 from 9 Y3: 3 from 9	Y1 3½ Y2 3 Y3 1	¾ ¾ ¾	1 1 0	Y1 no exams Y2 40% Y3 70%
BSc Comb. Hons modular degree ☆	3								
BSc Sing. Hons ☆	3								
Edge Hill College									
BA Comb. Hons in Applied SocSci (1/2 time in P.)	3	none	60	3	Y1: 1; Y2: 2; Y3: 1	Y1 6 Y2 10 Y3 8	4 5 5	0 0 RP	Y1 60% Y2 60% Y3 60%
BA Comb. Hons in Applied SocSci minor (1/4 time in P.)	3		15						

Edinburgh University

Course		Entrance			Requirements						
MA Sing. Hons	4	SCE or GCSE Maths (& SCE or GCSE Biology preferred)	}40	16	Ys 1-2: none; Y3: 4 from 8; Y4: 4 from 7	Y1 3	½	0	Y1 80%		
MA Comb. Hons w. Linguistics, Business Studies or Philosophy	4					Y2 3	0	3	Y2 60%		
BSc Sing. Hons in Biological Sciences	4		20			Y3 11	0	3	Y3 no exams		
BSc general degree in SocSci or Biological Sciences	3		60								

Exeter University

Course		Entrance			Requirements					
BSc Sing. Hons	3	GCSE Maths	18	15	Y1: none; Y2: none; Y3: 6 from 25	Y1 4	1-2	6	Y1 no exams	
BA Sing. Hons in SocSci	3		18			Y2 8	1-2	6	Y2 66%	
BA Sing. Hons in European Studies**	4		6			Y3 0	8	8	Y3 66%	
BA Comb. Hons w. Sociology	3		6							
BSc Comb. Hons w. Computer Science or Biology	3		12							

Glasgow College

Course		Entrance			Requirements					
BA Sing. Hons in SocSci (PSY)	4	none	18	12	Ys 1-3: none; Y4: 4 from 7	Y1 1½	¾	¾	Y1 60%	
BA Comb. Hons in SocSci (PSY) w. Sociology, Politics or Economics	4		6			Y2 2	½	11½	Y2 60%	
BA ordinary degree	3		20			Y3 2½	2½	2	Y3 75%	
						Y4 4	5	RP	Y4 60%	

Glasgow University

Course		Entrance			Requirements					
MA Sing. Hons	4	none	20	18	Ys 1-3: none; Y4: 4 from 15	Y1 3	0	3	Y1 100%	
MA Sing. Hons in SocSci	4		15			Y2 4	1	4	Y2 100%	
BSc Sing. Hons	4		15			Y3 8	0	6	Y3 100%	
MA ordinary degree	4		100			Y4 8	0	8	Y4 100%	
MA ordinary degree in SocSci	4		100							
BSc ordinary degree	3		100							

Title of course	No. of years	Special entry requirements	Student nos.	Staff nos.	Psychology options	Psychology contact hours per week			Percentage of each year's assessment attributed to formal exams
						Lectures	Seminars	Lab work	
Hatfield Polytechnic									
BSc Sing. Hons	3	GCSE Maths & Eng. Lang.	47	14	Ys 1-2: none; Y3: 6 from 10	Y1 10 Y2 10 Y3 8	4 3 1	5 6 RP	Y1 60% Y2 80% Y3 75%
Huddersfield Polytechnic									
BSc Comb. Hons w. Sociology	3	(GCSE Maths preferred)	45	10	Ys 1-2: none; Y3: 4 from 10	Y1 3 Y2 4 Y3 4	3 4 8	3 2 RP	Y1 60% Y2 48% Y3 56%
Hull University									
BSc Sing. Hons	3	GCSE Maths & Eng. Lang.	49	15	Y1: 2 from 12; Y2: 5 from 26; Y3: 8 from 32	Y1 12 Y2 9 Y3 2	1 1 7	5 5 3	Y1 82% Y2 79% Y3 44%
BSc Sing. Hons w. Occupational or Clinical Psychology	4		12						
BA Comb. Hons w. Sociology or Philosophy	3		3						
Humberside College									
BA Comb. Hons in Applied SocSci ☆	3	(GCSE Maths preferred)	85	13	Ys 1-2: none; Y3: 2 from 10	Y1 5 Y2 4 Y3 4	5 4 4	3 3 3	Y1 50% Y2 50% Y3 50%
BA Comb. Hons in Combined Studies ☆	3		60						
Keele University									
BA Comb. Hons w. 1 of poss. 18 other subjects (may include foundation year with subsidiary P.)	3 or 4	none	100	11	Y1: poss. foundation yr; Y2: none; Y3: 3 from 9; Y4: 1 from 10	Y1 Poss. FOUNDATION YR Y2 3 Y3 3 Y4 3	 1 1 1	 2 2 2	Y1 30% Y2 30% Y3 30% Y4 66%

University of Kent at Canterbury

Course			
BA Sing. Hons in Social P. ☆	3	63	
BA Sing. Hons in Applied	4	9	
Social P.** ☆	3	18	
BA Sing. Hons in Social & Educational P. ☆	3	1	
BA Sing. Hons in Applied	4	4	
Social & Educational P.** ☆	3	3	
BA Comb. Hons in Social P, Social Policy & Administration ☆	3	2	
BA Comb. Hons in Social P. & Social Anthropology ☆	3	1	
BA Sng. Hons in Social P. & Social Statistics, Philosophy or Industrial Relations ☆	3		

GCSE Maths

12

Ys 1-2: none; Y3: 4 from 16

Y1	4	2	2	Y1	90%
Y2	5	5	3	Y2	90%
Y3	5	5	RP	Y3	90%

Lancashire Polytechnic

Course			
BSc Sing. Hons	3	60	
BSc in Combined Studies	3	50	
BSc Comb. Hons w. Cognitive Science	3	10	
BSc Comb. Hons w. Neuroscience	3	10	

GCSE Maths

17

Ys 1-2: none; Y3: 8 from 25

Y1	6½	2½	2½	Y1	55%
Y2	5½	1½	6	Y2	75%
Y3	5	4	RP	Y3	75%

Lancaster University

Course			
BA or BSc Sing. Hons	3	50	
BA or BSc Comb. Hons w. Organizational Studies, Educational Studies, Linguistics, Marketing, Religious Studies, Sociology, Women's Studies	3	15	

GCSE Maths

18

Ys 1-2: none; Y3: 6 from 18

Y1	2	1	1	Y1	60%
Y2	4½	2½	2	Y2	no exams
Y3	4	2	RP	Y3	52% (av.)

Title of course	No. of years	Special entry requirements	Student nos.	Staff nos.	Psychology options	Psychology contact hours per week			Percentage of each year's assessment attributed to formal exams
						Lectures	Seminars	Lab-work	
Leeds University									
BSc Sing. Hons*	3		40	13	Ys 1-2: none; Y3: 3 from 4	Y1 3 Y2 7 Y3 6	1 1 6	3 6 6	Y1 66% Y2 65% Y3 70%
BSc Comb. Hons w. Computer Science	3		6						
BA Comb. Hons w. Management Studies	3	GCSE Maths	6						
BA Comb. Hons w. Philosophy	3		6						
BA Comb. Hons w. Sociology	3		6						
Leicester University									
BSc Sing. Hons	3	GCSE Maths or Statistics	30	13	Ys 1-2: none; Y3: 4 from 9	Y1 5 Y2 5 Y3 6	1 1 ½	1¾ 1¾ RP	Y1 77% Y2 77% Y3 67%
BA Comb. Hons w. Sociology, French or English ☆	3		30						
BSc Comb. Hons w. wide range of science, arts and social science subjects ☆	3								
Liverpool Polytechnic									
BSc Comb. Hons in Applied P. ☆	3	GCSE Maths	50	11	Ys 1-2: none; Y3: 3 from 9	Y1 1½ Y2 6 Y3 4	1 2 4	3 3 1	Y1 60% Y2 60% Y3 50%
Liverpool University									
BA Sing. Hons (w. wide range of social science and arts subjects)	3	GCSE Maths & Eng. Lang.	30	12	Ys 1-2: none; Y3: 5 from 12	Y1 6½ Y2 4¾ Y3 4	1½ ¾ 1½	1½-3¼ 1¼ RP	Y1 80% Y2 80% Y3 65%
BSc Sing. Hons (w. wide range of science subjects)	3	GCSE Maths & Eng. Lang. & 2 science A-Levels	15						

LONDON UNIVERSITY

Birkbeck College

Course	A-level	GCSE	Applied	Places	Entry	Y col 1	Y col 2	Y col 3	%
BSc Sing. Hons ☆	4	GCSE Maths	8	12	No info available	No info available			No info available
BSc Comb. Hons w. Biology, Maths or Physics ☆	4		72						
BA Comb. Hons w. Philosophy ☆ (all 3 part-time only)	4		2						

Goldsmiths' College

Course	A-level	GCSE	Applied	Places	Entry	Y col 1	Y col 2	Y col 3	%
BSc Sing. Hons * ☆	3	GCSE Maths	60	16	Ys 1-2: none; Y3: 6 from 18	Y1 5	Y1 2	Y1 3	Y1 100%
BSc Ccmb. Hons w. Anthropology ☆	3		10			Y2 8	Y2 1	Y2 3	Y2 100%
BSc Comb. Hons w. Maths	3		5			Y3 8	Y3 1	Y3 RP	Y3 70%
BSc Comb. Hons w. Computer Science	3		5						

London School of Economics

Course	A-level	GCSE	Applied	Places	Entry	Y col 1	Y col 2	Y col 3	%
BSc Sing. Hons in Social P.	3	GCSE Maths	20	9	Ys: 1-2: none; Y3: 4 from 16	Y1 6	Y1 4	Y1 3	Y1 0
BSc Econ Sing. Hons in Social P.	3		10			Y2 5	Y2 4	Y2 3	Y2 85%
						Y3 7	Y3 3	Y3 1	Y3 75%

Royal Holloway & Bedford New College

Course	A-level	GCSE	Applied	Places	Entry	Y col 1	Y col 2	Y col 3	%
BSc Sing. Hons	3	GCSE Maths or A-Level P.	40	8	Y1: none; Y2: 4 from 5; Y3: 7 from 14	Y1 6	Y1 1	Y1 5	Y1 100%
BSc Comb. Hons w. Maths	3		5			Y2 8	Y2 ½	Y2 5	Y2 100%
BSc Comb. Hons w. Statistics	3		5			Y3 7	Y3 1	Y3 2	Y3 87½%

University College

Course	A-level	GCSE	Applied	Places	Entry	Y col 1	Y col 2	Y col 3	%
BSc Sing. Hons	3	(GCSE Maths preferred)	63	27	Y1: 1; Y2: 2; Y3: 4 from 16	Y1 11	Y1 1	Y1 6	Y1 75%
BSc Comb. Hons w. Cognitive Science	3		15			Y2 10	Y2 1	Y2 7	Y2 67%
						Y3 6	Y3 2	Y3 RP	Y3 85%

Title of course	No. of years	Special entry requirements	Student nos.	Staff nos.	Psychology options	Psychology contact hours per week			Percentage of each year's assessment attributed to formal exams
						Lectures	Seminars	Lab work	
Loughborough University									
(Dept of Social Sciences) BSc Sing. Hons in Social P.	3	none	24	6	Y1: none; Y2: 3 from 8; Y3: 2 from 8	Y1 9 Y2 5 Y3 4	1½-2½ 2½ 2	3 3 RP	Y1 58% Y2 75% Y3 50%
(Dept of Human Sciences) BSc Sing. Hons in Human P.	3	GCSE Maths & Eng. Lang.	50	12	Ys 1-2: none; Y3: 3 from 8	Y1 10 Y2 10 Y3 9	1 5 2	6 0 0	Y1 46% Y2 50% Y3 62%
BSc Sing. Hons in Ergonomics**	4		72						
Manchester Polytechnic									
BSc Sing. Hons ☆	3	GCSE Maths & Eng. Lang.	50	18	Ys 1-2: none; Y3: 5 from 12	Y1 6½ Y2 5½ Y3 5	5 4½ 5	2½ 3 RP	Y1 46% Y2 50% Y3 62%
BSc Hons in Combined Studies	3		35						
Manchester University									
BSc Sing. Hons	3	GCSE Maths	44	22	Ys 1-2: none; Y3: 3 from 32	Y1 10 Y2 10 Y3 4	1 1 1	2 2 RP	Y1 60% Y2 56% Y3 36%
BA Sing. Hons	3		30						
Middlesex Polytechnic									
BA Sing. Hons in SocSci **	4	(GCSE Maths preferred)	28	19	Y1: none; Y2: 1 from 18; Y3: 5 from 18	Y1 4 Y2 5 Y3 5	4 5 5	3 3 3	Y1 0 Y2 50% Y3 75%
BSc Sing. Hons	3		50						
BA Comb. Hons w. Spanish **	4		10						
Nene College									
BA/BSc Comb. Hons w. 2 or 3 of poss. 28 other subjects	3	(GCSE Maths preferred)	35-40	6	Ys 1-3: none	Y1 3 Y2 3 Y3 6	½ ½ 2	3 3 RP	Y1 60% Y2 60% Y3 60%

Newcastle Polytechnic

BSc Sirg. Hons

Years	Entry requirements	Intake		Structure
3	GCSE Maths & Eng. Lang.	40	10	Ys 1-2: none; Y3: 4 from 21

	A	B	C	
Y1	5	5	3	100%
Y2	5	5	3	90%
Y3	3	7	1	80%

Newcastle University

Course	Years	Entry requirements	Intake		Structure
BSc Sing. Hons	3	} GCSE Maths	15	9	Ys 1-2: none; Y3: 5 from 16
BA Sing. Hons	3		15		
BA Comb. Hons w. up to 5 other arts or social science subjects	3		15		
BSc Joint Hons w. Maths, Statistics or Computing	3		10		

	A	B	C	
Y1	3	¼	2	65%
Y2	5	½	2½	80%
Y3	2½	(varies)	RP	75%

Nottingham University

Course	Years	Entry requirements	Intake		Structure
BA Sing. Hons*	3		21	20	Y1: none; Y2: 3 from 4 Y3: 6 from 23
BSc Sing. Hons*	3		12		
BSc Comb. Hons in Applied Cognitive Science*	3	} GCSE Maths	10		
BSc Comb. Hons in Behavioural Science*	3		3		
BSc Comb. Hons in Computer Science & Cognitive Science*	3		3		
BSc Comb. Hons w. Maths*	3		5		
BA Comb. Hons w. Philosophy*	3		4		
BA Comb. Hons w. Linguistics*	3				

	A	B	C	
Y1	4	2	3	no exams
Y2	9	4	3	82%
Y3	8	0	RP	40%

Open University

Course	Years	Entry requirements	Intake		Structure
BA Comb. Hons w. 1 of any other OU subject (☆ part-time only)	varies	none	200	20	Ys 1-4: modular structure

self-study + TV/audio projects, day schools and summer schools

Y1	50%
Y2	50%
Y3	50%

Title of course	No. of years	Special entry requirements	Student nos.	Staff nos.	Psychology options	Psychology contact hours per week			Percentage of each year's assessment attributed to formal exams
						Lectures	Seminars	Lab work	
Oxford Polytechnic									
BA Comb. Hons ☆	3	GCSE Maths/ internal test	40	9	Y1: none; Ys 2-3: modular structure	Y1 3	1	3	Y1 50%
BSc Comb. Hons ☆	3					Y2 6	2	6	Y2 50%
BEd Comb. Hons ☆	3					Y3 6	2	6 + RP	Y3 35%
(all with 1 of poss. 32 other subjects; type of degree depends on pattern of study on modular course)									
Oxford University									
BA Sing. Hons in Experimental P.	3	entry through individual colleges	35	19	Y1: none; Ys 2-3: 7 from 14	Y1 4	3	2	Y1 100%
BA Comb. Hons w. Philosophy & Physiology	3		35			Y2 6	2	3	Y2 87½%
						Y3 6	2	3 + RP	Y3 87½%
Portsmouth Polytechnic									
BSc Sing. Hons	3	GCSE Maths & 1 science A-Level	42	8	Ys 1-2: none; Y3: 3 from 7	Y1 9	2	3	Y1 no exams
						Y2 7	2	3	Y2 75%
						Y3 6	3	RP	Y3 86%
Reading University									
BA Sing. Hons	3	GCSE Maths	30	15	Ys 1-2: none; Y3: 2 from 12	Y1 3	0	3	Y1 70%
BA Comb. Hons w. Linguistics, Philosophy or Sociology	3		15			Y2 8	2	6	Y2 no exams
BA Comb. Hons w. Art	4					Y3 0	12	RP	Y3 60%
BSc Sing. Hons	3		20						
BSc Comb. Hons w. Cybernetics, Zoology or Maths	3		10						

College of Ripon & York St John

BA/BSc Comb. Hons w. 1 of poss. 16 other subjects ☆ — A-levels: 4 — Entry: none — 60 — 10

Ys 1-4: modular structure

Year				Assessment
Y1	4	2	0	no exams
Y2	4	2	0	no exams
Y3	4	2	0	20%
Y4	4	2		80%

Roehampton Institute of H.E.

BA/BSc Comb. Hons w. 1 of poss.13 other subjects — A-levels: 3 — Entry: GCSE Maths (& 1 science A-Level preferred) — 70 — 10

Y1: none; Ys 2-3: 3-4 from 8 options

Year				Assessment
Y1	2⅓	2⅓	2	70%
Y2	2⅓	2⅓	2	70%
Y3	3⅓	4	RP	50% (av.)

St Andrews University

MA Sing. Hons — A-levels: 4
MA Joint Hons w. 1 of 8 poss. other subjects — A-levels: 4 — Entry: none — 20
other subjects — 3
BSc Joint Hons w. 1 of 5 poss. other subjects — A-levels: 4
other subjects
BSc Sing. Hons — A-levels: 4 — 16

14

Ys 1-2: none; Ys 3-4: 8 from 14

Year				Assessment
Y1	2½	0	1⅓	40%
Y2	2½	⅓	1⅓	40%
Y3	4	2	⅓	no exams
Y4	1⅓	⅓	RP	70%

Sheffield University

BSc Sing. Hons — A-levels: 3 — 18
BA Sing. Hons — A-levels: 3 — 34
BA Comb. Hons w. Sociology — A-levels: 3 — 4
BA Comb. Hons w. Philosophy — A-levels: 3 — 2

Entry: GCSE Maths — 16

Ys 1-3: none

Year				Assessment
Y1	2	⅔	3	100%
Y2	6	⅓	4	100%
Y3	5	¼+	RP	63%

Polytechnic South West

BSc Sing. Hons* — A-levels: 3 — 70
BSc Comb. Hons w. 1 of poss. 11 other subjects — A-levels: 3 — 30

Entry: GCSE Maths & Eng. Lang. — 21

Y1: none; Y2: 1; Y3: 4 from 20

Year				Assessment
Y1	7	1	3	100%
Y2	7	1	3	75%
Y3	1	8	3	55%

Title of course	No. of years	Special entry requirements	Student nos.	Staff nos.	Psychology options	Psychology contact hours per week			Percentage of each year's assessment attributed to formal exams
						Lectures	Seminars	Lab work	
Southampton University									
BSc Sing. Hons ☆	3		⎰ 10	14	Y1: none;	Y1 10	3	3	Y1 65%
BSc Comb. Hons w. Physiology	3	GCSE Maths	⎱		Y2: 6 from 7;	Y2 8	4	3	Y2 70%
BSc Sing. Hons in SocSci	3		25		Y3: 2 from 15	Y3 2	4	RP	Y3 60%
BSc Comb. Hons w. Sociology	3		8						
Stirling University									
BA/BSc general degree w. major in P. ☆	3	(GCSE Maths preferred)	20	17	Ys 1-2: none;	Y1 9	2	4	Y1 50%
BA/BSc Sing. Hons	4		35		Y3: 6 from 11;	Y2 6	6	8	Y2 50%
BA/BSc Comb. Hons w. 11 poss. other subjects	4		15		Y4: 3 from 16	Y3 6	6	8	Y3 50%
						Y4 5	6	3+RP	Y4 30%
Strathclyde University									
BA Sing. Hons* ☆	4		20	13	Ys 1-2: none;	Y1 2	½	¼	Y1 75%
BA Comb. Hons* ☆	4	none	10		Y3: 4 from 6;	Y2 4	1	1	Y2 67%
BA ordinary degree ☆	3		20		Y4: 8 from 13	Y3 4	2½	1¼	Y3 67%
						Y4 3	6	RP	Y4 80% (av.)
Sunderland Polytechnic									
BA Hons in Combined Studies ☆	3	(GCSE Maths preferred)	140	7	Y1: none;	Y1 3	3	1	Y1 60%
BA Comb. Hons in SocSci	3		35		Y2: 3 from 4;	Y2 3	3	1	Y2 60%
BA Comb. Hons in Communication Studies	3		60		Y3: 2 from 5	Y3 ⅔	⅔	RP	Y3 60%

Surrey University

Course		Entry		
BSc Sing. Hons**	4	GCSE Maths or Statistics (& 1 quantitative A-level preferred)	25	15
BSc Comb. Hons w. Sociology**	4		25	

Ys 1-2: none; Y3: placement; Y4: 3 from 7

Y1	6	1½	1⅔	no exams
Y2	5⅔	2¼	2½	70%
Y3	PLACEMENT			no exams
Y4	1⅔	6⅓	RP	70%

Sussex University

(Dept of Psychology)

Course		Entry		
BA in Social P.	3	none	30	18
BA in Developmental P.	3		30	
BA in P. & Computer Models	3		10	

(all 3 involve 60%-70% P.)

Ys 1-2: none; Y3: 2 from 12

Y1	1½	1¾	1¾	no exams
Y2	¾	1¾	2¾	50%
Y3	0	1¼	RP	50%

(Lab of Experimental Psychology)

Course		Entry		
BSc Sing. Hons	3	none	40	10

Ys 1-2: none; Y3: 4 from 16

Y1	9	3	4	10%
Y2	6	2	4	25%
Y3	6	3	RP	60%

Trinity and All Saints' College

Course		Entry		
BA Comb. Hons w. Business Management & Administration**	3	(GCSE Maths preferred)	12-15	6
BA Comb. Hons w. Public Media**	3		12-15	

Ys 1-2: none; Y3: 3-4 from 5

Y1	range of 3	3	3	70%
Y2	workshops	3	3	70%
Y3	etc.	RP	RP	70%

University of Ulster

Course		Entry		
BSc Sing. Hons in Applied P. * ☆	4	GCSE Maths & Eng. Lang.	35	31
BSc Comb. Hons w. Computing	4		15	
BSc Comb. Hons in Social P. w. Sociology**	3		35	
BSc Comb. Hons in Occupational P. *	4		20	

Ys 1-2: none; Y3: placement; Y4: 5 from 10+

Y1	6	5	3	50%
Y2	5	3	8	70%
Y3	PLACEMENT			60%
y4	6	6	4	60%

Title of course	No. of years	Special entry requirements	Student nos.	Staff nos.	Psychology options	Psychology contact hours per week			Percentage of each year's assessment attributed to formal exams
						Lectures	Seminars	Lab work	
Polytechnic of Wales									
BSc Comb. Hons in Behavioural Science	3	(GCSE Maths or Statistics preferred)	40	12	Ys 1-2: none; Y3: 4 from 12	Y1 7 Y2 7 Y3 5	Y1 3 Y2 3 Y3 5	Y1 5 Y2 5 Y3 RP	Y1 67% Y2 52% Y3 64%
UNIVERSITY OF WALES									
University College of North Wales									
BA/BSc Sing. Hons	3	(GCSE Maths preferred)	35	12	Ys 1-2: none; Y3: 5 from 8	Y1 4 Y2 6 Y3 5	Y1 1½ Y2 ⅔ Y3 1⅓	Y1 ¾ Y2 1 Y3 RP	Y1 75% Y2 100% Y3 60%
BA Comb. Hons w. Education, Physical Education, Linguistics, Sociology or Social Administration	3		} 10						
BSc Comb. Hons w. Maths or Biochemistry	3								
University College of Swansea									
BA Sing. Hons	3	GCSE Maths (+ special requirements for individual degrees)	18	10	Y1: none; Ys 2-3: 16 from 30	Y1 4 Y2 8 Y3 8	Y1 ½ Y2 2 Y3 2	Y1 3 Y2 4 Y3 RP	Y1 80% Y2 90% Y3 75%
BSc Sing. Hons	3		23						
BSc Joint Hons w. Biological Sciences	3		6						
BSc Econ Joint Hons w. 1 of poss. 4 other subjects	3		17						
BSc Econ Comb. Hons w. 1 of poss. 6 other subjects	3		5						

University of Wales College of Cardiff

(Dept of Psychology)

Course	Yrs	Places	Entry req.	Options	Yr				Assessment
BA Sing. Hons	3	30	GCSE Maths (22)	Ys 1-2: none; Y3: largely option-based	Y1	6	3	5	100%
BA Comb. Hons w. Humanities, English, Philosophy or Education	3	10			Y2	8	10	5	no exams
BSc Sing. Hons in Applied P.	3	14			Y3		3	3	RP
BSc (Tech) Sing. Hons in Applied P.*	4	27							
BSc Comb. Hons w. Physiology	3	10							
BSc Econ Comb. Hons w. Sociology	3	10							

(School of Education)

Course	Yrs	Places	Entry req.	Options	Yr			Assessment
BA Sing. Hons in Education	3	5	none (3)	Ys 1-3: none	Y1	4	varies	100%
BA Comb. Hons in Education w. P.	3	20			Y2	8		100%
					Y3	8		60%

Warwick University

Course	Yrs	Places	Entry req.	Options	Yr				Assessment
BSc Sing. Hons	3	30	GCSE Maths (13)	Ys 1-2: none; Y3: numerous	Y1	1⅓	⅔	1	50%
BA Comb. Hons w. Education	3	10			Y2	2⅔	1⅓	RP	40%
BA Comb. Hons w. Philosophy	3	5			Y3	2⅔	0	RP	25%

West London Institute

Course	Yrs	Places	Entry req.	Options	Yr				Assessment
BSc/BA Comb. Hons in Sport Studies	3	60	2 science GCSEs (3)	Y1: 2 from 4; Y2: 2 from 4; Y3: 2 from 8	Y1	1	1	1	40%
					Y2	1	1	RP	50%
					Y3	2	2	RP	40%

Title of course	No. of years	Special entry requirements	Student nos.	Staff nos.	Psychology options	Psychology contact hours per week			Percentage of each year's assessment attributed to formal exams
						Lectures	Seminars	Lab work	
Wolverhampton Polytechnic									
BA in Social Sciences	3	} none	100	9	Ys 1-3: modular structure	Y1 4	1	1	Y1 varies
BSc in Applied Sciences	3		45			Y2 10	2½	2½	Y2
BA in Comb. Studies (type of degree depends on pattern of study on modular course)	3		20			Y3 14	3½	3½	Y3
Worcester College of H.E.									
BSc Hons in Combined Studies	3	} none	20	6	Ys 1-2: none; Y3: 1 from 2	Y1 2	1⅓	1	Y1 60%
BA (SocSci) Comb. Hons w. 3 from wide range of subjects	3		20			Y2 1⅓	1	1	Y2 60%
BEd Comb. Hons	3	GCSE Maths & Eng. Lang.	100			Y3 1	1⅔	RP	Y3 60%
York University									
BSc/BA Sing. Hons	3	GCSE Maths or Statistics	40	12	Ys 1-2: none; Y3: 4 from 24	Y1 4	2	3	Y1 no exams
						Y2 4	2	3	Y2 90%
						Y3 0	6	RP	Y3 40%
EIRE									
Trinity College									
BA (MOD) Sing. Hons	4	} none	15	6	Ys 1-3: none; Y4: 4 from 9	Y1 4	1	6	Y1 75%
BA (MOD) Comb. Hons	4		10			Y2 4	2	3	Y2 69%
						Y3 4	2	RP	Y3 84%
						Y4 4	1	RP	Y4 75%

University College (Cork)

Course		Requirements			Structure	Y1/Y2/Y3				Exams Y1/Y2/Y3
BA Sing. Hons ☆	3	none	30	8	Ys 1-2: none; Y3: 4 from 8	Y1 5 / Y2 8 / Y3 7	1 / 1 / 2	2 / / RP		Y1 no exams / Y2 80% / Y3 80%
BSc Sing. Hons	3		2							

University College Dublin

Course		Requirements			Structure	Y1/Y2/Y3				Exams Y1/Y2/Y3
BA Sing. Hons	3	Eng. Lang & 1 foreign language	1*0	10	Y1 none; Ys 2-3: modular structure	Y1 4 / Y2 12 / Y3 12	1 / 1 / 1	0 / 9 / RP		Y1 100% / Y2 80% / Y3 80%
BSc Sing. Hons (w. Maths, Pharmacology or Computer Science)	4		5							

University College (Galway)

Course		Requirements			Structure	Y1/Y2/Y3				Exams Y1/Y2/Y3
BA Sing. Hons	3	(SSLC Maths & Biology preferred)	25	4	Ys 1-3: none	Y1 3 / Y2 12 / Y3 12	1 / 2 / 2	2 / 4 / 4+RP		Y1 75% / Y2 70% / Y3 70%

Table B

Institution	Research Areas	Postgraduate Qualifications by Courses in Psychology
Aberdeen University Dept of Psychology King's College Old Aberdeen AB9 2UB tel. (0224) 272238	Perception and memory for faces; brain evoked potentials and visual perception; cross-cultural studies of cognitive processes	
Aston University Dept of Organizational Studies & Applied Psychology Business School Birmingham B4 7ET tel. (021) 359 3611 x4915	Sustained attention (individual differences); stress (vehicle drivers); human-machine interaction	
Bath University School of Social Sciences Claverton Down Bath BA2 7AY tel. (0225) 826826 x5278	Economic psychology; health psychology; adolescent development	
Queen's University of Belfast Dept of Psychology Belfast BT7 1NN tel. (0232) 661111 x4360	Psychopharmacology; psychological aspects of disability; social psychology	MSc Abnormal P. MSc Developmental and Educational P. MSc Occupational P.

Birmingham University
School of Psychology
PC Box 363
Birmingham B29 7PH
tel. (021) 414 4931

Applied social psychology
psychopharmacology; clinical and
health psychology

MSc Clinical P.
MSc Cognitive Science
Dip. Social Learning Theory

Bolton Institute of H.E.
Dept of Psychology &
Health Studies
Deane Road
Bolton BL3 5AB
tel. (0204) 28851 x3140

Applied animal behaviour
(captive environments); cognitive
psychology (decision making);
social-developmental psychology
(health behaviour)

MSc Applied P.

Bristol University
Dept of Psychology
8-10 Berkeley Square
Bristol BS8 1HH
tel. (0272) 303030 xM335

Social psychology; perception;
cognitive psychology

Brunel University
Dept of Human Sciences
Uxbridge UB8 3PH
tel. (0895) 56461 x244

Cognitive psychology: psychology
of health and illness; visual processing

MSc Intelligent Systems

Buckingham University
School of Biological Sciences
Buckingham MK18 1EG
tel. (0280) 814080

ageing, individual differences;
ethology

Dip. in Psychotherapy

Institution	Research Areas	Postgraduate Qualifications by Courses in Psychology
Cambridge University Dept of Experimental Psychology Downing Street Cambridge CB2 3EB tel. (0223) 333550	Perception; psycholinguistics and cognition; developmental psychology	
Central London Polytechnic School of Paramedical Studies 115 New Cavendish Street London W1M 8JS tel. (01) 486 5811 x6373	Clinical psychology; memory; acoustics	
Chester College of H.E. Dept of Psychology Cheyney Road Chester CH1 4BJ tel. (0224) 375444	Psychology and education; vision and computers in psychology; ageing	
City of London Polytechnic Dept of Psychology Calcutta House Old Castle Street London E1 7NT tel. (01) 283 1030 x513	Psychopharmacology (depression, feeding); reading, spelling and memory in children; skills and human performance (human–computer interaction, decision making)	Dip P.

City University
Psychology Division
Dept of Social Science &
Humanities
Northampton Square
London EC1V 0HB
tel. (01) 253 4399 x4535

Memory and cognition; learning and
psychobiology; health psychology

Coventry Polytechnic
Dept of Social Science &
Policy Studies
Priory Street
Coventry CV1 5FB
tel. (0203) 224166 x2491

Self-concept in women; the elderly;
cognitive processes

**Crewe & Alsager College
of H.E.**
Dept of Sport & Human Science
Hassall Road
Alsager
Stoke-on-Trent ST7 2HL
tel. (0270) 88250 x3063

Health psychology; sports psychology;
social psychology

Dundee University
Dept of Psychology
Dundee DD1 4HN
tel. (0382) 23181 x4623

Cognitive psychology/cognitive science;
social psychology; perception and
performance

Dip P. of Reading

Institution	Research Areas	Postgraduate Qualifications by Courses in Psychology
Durham University Dept of Psychology Science Laboratories Durham DH1 3LE tel. (091) 374 2610	Cognition and cognitive science; medical and health psychology; neuroscience (brain and behaviour)	
Ealing College of H.E. Psychology Division St Mary's Road London W5 5RF tel. (01) 579 4111 x3224	Spina bifida; opinion polls; language and social power	
Polytechnic of East London Dept of Psychology Romford Road London E15 4LZ tel. (01) 590 7722 x4186	Eyewitness testimony; psychological aspects of AIDS; media and TV research	MSc Clinical P. MSc Educational P. MSc Occupational and Organizational P. MSc Counselling P.
Edge Hill College Dept of Applied Social Sciences St Helens Road Ormskirk L39 4US tel. (0695) 75171 x205	Adolescent behaviour problems and delinquency; parenting styles and family demographic variables; friendship patterns and disclosures in speech	

Edinburgh University
Dept of Psychology
7 George Square
Edinburgh EH8 9JZ
tel. (031) 667 1011 x4418

Developmental psychology (especially young babies); language (especially in children); cognitive psychology

MPhil Clinical P.
MPhil Education

Exeter University
Dept of Psychology
Washington Singer Laboratories
Queen's Drive
Exeter EX4 4QG
tel. (0392) 264626

Social psychology; cognitive psychology economic psychology

MSc Clinical P.

Glasgow College
Dept of Psychology
Cowcaddens Road
Glasgow G4 0BA
tel. (041) 332 7090 x245

Psychology of witness testimony; decision making; education and gender

Glasgow University
Dept of Psychology
56 Hillhead Street
Glasgow G12 0BA
tel. (041) 339 8855 x5142

Cognitive psychology; cognitive science; addictions; psychophysiology (stress)

Hatfield Polytechnic
Psychology Division
College Lane
Hatfield AL10 9AB
tel. (07072) 79000 x4830

Cognitive psychology; neuropsychology; developmental psychology

MSc Occupational P.

Institution	Research Areas	Postgraduate Qualifications by Couses in Psychology
Huddersfield Polytechnic Dept of Behavioural Sciences Queensgate Huddersfield HD1 3DH tel. (0484) 22288 x2265	Evaluation research; special educational needs; decision making	MSc Analysis of Decision Processes
Hull University Dept of Psychology Hull HU6 7RX tel. (0482) 465546 x5933	Occupational psychology; clinical psychobiology; educational technology	MSc Clinical P. MSc Industrial P.
Humberside College School of Social and Professional Sudies Inglemire Avenue Hull HU6 7LU tel. (0482) 440550 x4087	Intergroup relations; mental handicap; depression and social isolation	
Keele University Dept of Psychology Keele ST5 5BG tel. (0782) 621111 x4401	Mental handicap; written communication; psychology of music	Dip/MA CommunityCare (Mental Handicap)

University of Kent at Canterbury
Institute of Social & Applied Psychology
Canterbury CT2 7LZ
tel. (0227) 764000 x3839

Social psychology and law; group processes and intergroup behaviour; social psychology of mental handicap

Lancashire Polytechnic
School of Psychology
Preston PR1 2TQ
tel. (0772) 201201 x2101

Psychobiology/neuroscience; cognitive psychology; developmental psychology

Lancaster University
Dept of Psychology
Lancaster LA1 4YF
tel. (0524) 65201 x3575

Cognitive psychology; developmental psychology; social psychology

Leeds University
Dept of Psychology
Leeds LS2 9JT
tel. (0532) 335724

Developmental and clinical psychology; applied social psychology; biological psychology

Leicester University
Dept of Psychology
University Road
Leicester LE1 7RH
tel. (0533) 522157

Clinical/abnormal psychology; cognitive/neuropsychology; developmental/social psychology

MSc Clinical P.
Dip Social Learning Theory/Practice

Institution	Research Areas	Postgraduate Qualifications by Courses in Psychology
Liverpool Polytechnic Section of Psychology Dept of Humanities & Social Science C. F. Mott Campus Liverpool Road Prescot L34 1NP tel. (051) 489 6201	Behaviourism, methodology and practice; human knowledge representation and knowledge engineering: humanistic psychology	
Liverpool University Dept of Psychology PO Box 147 Liverpool L69 3BX tel. (051) 794 6916	Neural mechanisms of behaviour; behavioural changes in ageing; social psychology of compliance	
LONDON UNIVERSITY		
Birkbeck College Dept of Psychology Malet Street London WC1E 7HX tel. (01) 580 6622 x312	Cognitive psychology and neuropsychology; social and abnormal psychology; physiological psychology and psychopharmacology	MSc Cognitive Neuropsychology MA Philosophy and P. of Language
Goldsmith's College Dept of Psychology New Cross London SE14 6NW tel. (01) 692 7171 x2022	Cognitive psychology and neuropsychology; selection methods of performance appraisal; counselling	MSc Counselling Dip. Cognitive Psychotherapy

London School of Economics
Dept of Social Psychology
Houghton Street
London WC2A 2AE
tel. (01) 405 7686 x2712

Psychology of social issues (energy, leisure, black youth); social cognition; health psychology

MSc Social P.

Royal Holloway & Bedford New College
Dept of Psychology
Egham Hill
Egham TW20 0EX
tel. (0784) 4 34455 x3526

Cognitive factors in anxiety; cognitive neuropsychology; driving behaviour

University College
Dept of Psychology
Gower Street
London WC1E 6BT
tel. (01) 387 7050 x5333

Cognition (vision, language, speech); medical and clinical psychology; human-computer interaction

MSc Clinical P.
MSc Educational P.
MSc Ergonomics
MSc Experimental P.

Loughborough University
Dept of Social Sciences
Loughborough LE11 3TU
tel. (0509) 263171 x3368

Social psychology: applied social psychology and social problems; analysis of language, discourse, and rhetoric

Dip/MA Women's Studies

Dept of Human Sciences
Loughborough LE11 3TU
tel. (0509) 263171 x3034

Organizational psychology; sleep; psychoacoustics

MSc Ergonomics

Institution	Research Areas	Postgraduate Qualifications by Courses in Psychology
Manchester Polytechnic Dept of Psychology & Speech Pathology Elizabeth Gaskell Hathersage Road Manchester M13 0JA tel. (061) 225 9054 x252	HIV and intravenous drug taking; interpersonal skills in nursing; legibility	
Manchester University Dept of Psychology Manchester M13 9PL tel. (061) 275 2585	Cognitive psychology; developmental psychology; social psychology	MSc Cognitive Science1
Middlesex Polytechnic School of Psychology Queensway Enfield EN3 4SF tel. (01) 368 1299 x2361	Health psychology and psychophysiology; cognitive psychology; social issues (e.g. gender)	MSc PGD P. and Health.
Nene College Dept of Psychology Park Campus Moulton Park Northampton NN2 7AL tel. (0604) 715000 x371	Temporal inference in young children; cross-national social attitudes survey research; applications of Buddhist psychology to helping professionals	

Newcastle Polytechnic
Dept of Health & Behavioural
Science
Ellison Place
Newcastle upon Tyne NE1 8ST
tel. (091) 232 6002 x4266

Health psychology; cognitive
psychology; sports psychology

MSc Educational P.

Newcastle University
Dept of Psychology
Newcastle upon Tyne NE1 7RU
tel. (091) 232 8511

Sociobiology; risk/subjective probability;
perception

Nottingham University
Dept of Psychology
University Park
Nottingham NG7 2RD
tel. (0602) 484848 x3182

Developmental psychology (disability,
instruction); applied psychology (stress,
unemployment, accidents); cognitive
science (face recognition, memory,
knowledge elicitation, expert systems,
human-machine interaction)

MSc Child P.
Dip Applied P.

Open University
Dept of Psychology
Milton Keynes MK7 6AA
tel. (0908) 653591

Cognitive psychology (including
biological aspects); social and
developmental psychology; artificial
intelligence

Oxford Polytechnic
Psychology Unit
Dept of Social Studies
Gipsy Lane
Headington
Oxford OX3 0BP
tel. (0865) 819750

Aggression and violence; nutrition and
brain development; evaluation in higher
education

Institution	Research Areas	Postgraduate Qualifications by Courses in Psychology
Oxford University Dept of Experimental Psychology South Parks Road Oxford OX1 3UD tel. (0865) 271444	Human experimental psychology; physiological psychology and animal behaviour; social psychology and behaviour disorders	
Portsmouth Polytechnic Dept of Psychology King Charles Street Portsmouth PO1 2ER tel. (0705) 827681 x730	Mental handicap; hypnosis; psychology and information technology	Dip/MSc Research Methods in P.
Reading University Dept of Psychology Earley Gate Whiteknights Reading RG6 2AL tel. (0734) 318523	Experimental and cognitive psychology; biological bases of behaviour (including psychopharmacology); social, abnormal and developmental psychology	
College of Ripon & York St John Dept of Social Science Lord Mayor's Walk York YO3 7EX tel. (0904) 656771	Small groups; adolescence; criminality	

Roehampton Institute of H.E.
Dept of Psychology
Digby Stuart College
Roehampton Lane
London SW15 5PH
tel. (01) 876 8273 x2258

Social cognition; mental health policy
and counselling; social knowledge;
unemployment and divorce

MSc Psychological Counselling

St Andrews University
Dept of Psychology
St Andrews
Fife KY16 9JU
tel. (0334) 76161 x7142

Neuropsychology; cognitive psychology;
primate psychology

MLitt Philosophy and P.
Dip Neuropsychology

Sheffield University
Dept of Psychology
Sheffield S10 2TN
tel. (0742) 768555 x6545

Cognitive science and artificial intelligence;
behavioural neuroscience; child
development and health psychology

MSc Occupational P.
MSc Educational P.

Polytechnic South West
Dept of Psychology
Drake Circus
Plymouth PL4 8AA
tel. (0752) 233157/8

Cognitive psychology; clinical psychology;
individual differences

MSc Clinical P.
MSc Intelligent Systems

Southampton University
Dept of Psychology
Southampton SO9 5NH
tel. (0703) 595000 x2612

Health psychology; cognitive psychology;
social and developmental psychology

MSc Educational P.

Institution	Research Areas	Postgraduate Qualifications by Courses in Psychology
Stirling University Dept of Psychology Stirling FK9 4LA tel. (0786) 73171 x2450	Developmental psychology; cognition and neuropsychology; applications of psychology to medicine	MSc P.
Strathclyde University Dept of Psychology 155 George Street Glasgow G1 1RD tel. (041) 552 4400 x2581	Social development; addiction studies; educational psychology	MSc Educational P. MSc Research Methods in Developmental and Social P.
Sunderland Polytechnic School of Social Studies Douro House Douro Terrace Sunderland SR2 7EE tel. (091) 515 2201	Social psychology; cognitive psychology; counselling psychology	
Surrey University Dept of Psychology Guildford GU2 5XH tel. (0483) 509175	Environmental psychology; social and developmental psychology; cognitive psychology	MSc Clinical P. MSc Environmental P. MSc Health P.

Sussex University
Dept of Psychology
Arts Building
Falmer
Brighton BN1 9QN
tel. (0273) 606755 x8030

Social psychology; cognitive psychology; developmental psychology

MSc Experimental P.

Laboratory of Experimental Psychology
Brighton BN1 9QG
tel. (0273) 606755 x8058

Hearing and speech; artificial intelligence and cognition; physiological psychology

Trinity and All Saints' College
Dept of Psychology
Brownberrie Lane
Horsforth
Leeds LS18 5HD
tel. (0532) 584341 x303

Language and cognitive development; reasoning and decision making; repertory gric technique and special educational needs

University of Ulster
(Coleraine site)
Department of Psychology
Cromore Road
Coleraine BT52 1FA
tel. (0265) 44141

Individual differences; social psychology and conflict in Northern Ireland; behavioural analysis and biology

University of Ulster
(Jordanstown site)
Department of Psychology
Shore Road
Newtownabbey BT37 0QB
tel. (0232) 365131

Institution	Research Areas	Postgraduate Qualifications by Courses in Psychology
Polytechnic of Wales Dept of Behavioural & Communications Studies Pontypridd CF37 1DL tel. (0443) 480480	Gambling; health psychology; alcohol and behaviour	
UNIVERSITY OF WALES		
University College of **North Wales** Dept of Psychology Bangor LL57 2DG tel. (0248) 351151 x2201	Human learning; health psychology; cognitive psychology (and dyslexia)	
University College of Swansea Dept of Psychology Singleton Park Swansea SA2 8PP tel. (0792) 295278	Neuropsychology; occupational psychology; applied cognitive psychology	
University of Wales College **of Cardiff** School of Psychology PO Box 901 Cardiff CF1 3YG tel. (0222) 874000 x4007	Cognitive ergonomics and cognitive neuroscience; social relations and human development; health psychology	MSc Occupational P. MSc Applied P. (Ergonomics/ Training/Instruction) MScApplied Social P.
School of Education PO Box 78 Cardiff CF1 1XL tel. (0222) 874000 x4459	Personality and personal development; special education; language development	

Warwick University
Dept of Psychology
Coventry CV4 7AL
tel. (0203) 523189

Sensory psychology; cognitive psychology;
developmental and social psychology

MSc Psychotherapy
MSc Cognition and Computing

West London Institute
Dept of Human & Environmental
Sciences
Borough Road
Isleworth TW7 5DU
tel. (01) 568 8741

Interpersonal relations in sport;
relaxation techniques in sport;
psychological intervention in sport

Wolverhampton Polytechnic
Psychology Section
Centre for Health Sciences
62-68 Lichfield Street
Wolverhampton WV1 1DJ
tel. (0902) 28525

Designing instructional text; applied
cognitive psychology; counselling
psychology

Dip/MSc Applications of P.

Worcester College of H.E.
Psychology Section
Henwick Grove
Worcester WR2 6AJ
tel. (0905) 748080

Organizational behaviour; educational
psychology (educational technology,
gifted children); methods of instruction

York University
Dept of Psychology
York YO1 5DD
tel. (0904) 430000 x3189

Personality, development and social
behaviour; applied psychology and
real-world problems (clinical, computing);
perceptual and cognitive abilities
of humans and animals

Institution	Research Areas	Postgraduate Qualifications by Courses in Psychology
EIRE		
Trinity College Dept of Psychology Dublin 2 tel. (0001) 772941	Safety in transport; child development; history of psychology	MCoun P.
University College (Cork) Dept of Applied Psychology Cork tel. (010 353 021) 276871 x2101	Psychology and law; human-computer interaction: cognitive psychology	MCoun Counselling DCG Careers Guidance Dip. P.
University College Dublin Dept of Logic & Psychology Belfield Dublin 4 tel. (0001) 693244	Women's issues; social and vocational issues; selection of apprentices	
University College (Galway) Dept of Psychology Galway tel. (010 353 091) 64245	Psychology of mental, physical and educational handicap; counselling psychology (especially AIDS victims and suicidal clients); cognitive processes	

Abbreviations

Comb. Hons	:	Combined Honours degree
info.	:	information
P.	:	Psychology
poss.	:	possible
RP	:	research project
Sing. Hons	:	Single Honours degree
SocSci	:	Social Sciences
SSLC	:	Secondary School Leaving Certificate
w.	:	with
*	:	optional sandwich component
**	:	obligatory sandwich component
☆	:	degree that can be studied on a part-time basis